Hippie to Mystic

iUniverse, Inc.
New York   Bloomington

Hippie to Mystic

iUniverse books may be ordered through booksellers or by contacting:

iUniverse
1663 Liberty Drive
Bloomington, IN 47403
www.iuniverse.com
1-800-Authors (1-800-288-4677)

ISBN: 978-1-4401-4504-9(pbk)
ISBN: 978-1-4401-4503-2 (ebk)

Printed in the United States of America

iUniverse rev. date: 6/10/2009

Hippie to Mystic

By Stanley (Dyal) Roberts

" … I give special thanks to Heaven, which raises the poor up from the dunghill and makes wise men out of fools."

Don Quixote

Table of Contents

Preface

I grew up in Southern Indiana. Poor, though I didn't realize it until high school. My father was the town bully, though thankfully, he left for good when I was in the seventh grade. I was raised by three good people: my mother, Iola Roberts; my grandmother, Urner Burlison; and my uncle, A L Burlison.

I was a math whiz, marbles champion, artist, and incredibly athletic for my age.

Now, some earlier experiences that helped mold my character. Starting with when my family (six kids and mother), moved in with grandma for the final time in 1957. Shortly after arriving, I went for a walk, remembering a playground from a previous visit. I was twelve but looked much older. Found the playground, as they were choosing sides for a football game. One boy asked if I wanted to play. I was probably the youngest. There were some fifteen on a side, with part of the field in gravel. I stepped in at defensive safety, as all other positions were taken. A very powerful looking man in his mid-twenties ran the ball. He was very quick and coordinated, outweighing me by some eighty pounds. Most were afraid to even try to tackle him, and those that tried, he easily out ran or out maneuvered. Then I was the only one left. He ran fast around me, but I dived, grabbing his leg, and bringing him down.

Before the next play, I was warned to be careful of him, as he had just gotten out of prison for armed robbery. Spontaneously, my adolescent brain starts racing a mile a minute, trying to figure out what to do. If I back down, then I'll be branded a coward. Yet, I don't want to get seriously hurt. It seems highly improbable I could stand up to him in a fight. Maybe he won't run the ball, or maybe someone else will get to him before he gets to me. He does run the ball again, and again I am the last obstacle. My brain is empty—there's no solution. He's charging towards me even faster that before. My reflexes take over. I run towards him. He cuts and is almost by me. I dive and barely grab his ankle, tripping him to the ground. From then on, I was the only one he didn't pick on. But I avoided him—intuitively not wanting to be connected to a life so full of violence. Later, I heard that he had killed at least one person.

When puberty set, romance was difficult as I was bashful and had little money and no car. Then a beautiful girl invited me to her apartment. She was liberated at fifteen because of her horrible home life. I dressed in my best clothes, was ready to leave, but something held me back. Later I heard that two guys had come to see her, and one had knifed the other. I didn't try to see her after that, as it really wasn't love. She was just beautiful and I was a teenager.

Mother said I had the taste of a rich man but the pocket of a poor man. I always reached for quality—it seems the best way to live. In the Navy in Pensacola, Florida, I took one month's pay and hitchhiked to New Orleans, got a cheap room for the weekend, and stocked up on white bread, baloney, and mustard. Walking around Bourbon Street, I chanced upon the Preservation Hall Jazz Band practicing. Later I met some nurses, got a date, and reserved a good table at Pete Fountain's. My date, the next day, took me on a grand tour of New Orleans. Then I hitchhiked back to Pensacola and ate the free food at the base, as my weekend cost all of that month's pay.

Once, when I was very young, some relatives we rarely saw came to visit. To me, they seemed wealthy. They wouldn't look at me, and seemed to leave in a hurry. Maybe they were afraid if they stayed longer they'd have to help us. I decided then-and-there that I would never be like them, for they seemed so empty. I would always be real, no matter what the consequence.

While in college at Indiana University, on the surface my life seemed perfect, but on the inside a nagging uneasiness pervaded. I had a wonderful girlfriend and great party friends—was even taking my first Yoga class, but, feeling the emptiness inside, I deeply surrendered, searching for an answer. After about half an hour there came emptiness … then a dream of playing basketball. I went to the gym, and after five hours of intense basketball my mind was once again clear and calm. In retrospect, I had been ignoring part of my essential nature. These were some of the experiences that helped form my early character, but, as this book will show, there is much more.

As time passed, different people mentioned to me that stories of my experiences were worth writing down. Once, reflecting on what I had to contribute to the world, it came to me that many others had achieved greater depth, but my wide range was somewhat unique. And I had written some poetry, so thought I could write. So, this book may be what I have to naturally contribute, for it's what we give that fulfills us, not what we take.

The spiritual part of this book doesn't start 'till mention of Yogi Bhajan at the end of chapter three, so if you are so inclined, you can start there. I am sometimes envious of those who have enough strength of character and depth of perception to not need experiences like the damaging ones of my early years.

Because of my outlook and interests, most of my friends were middle-class. I was recruited to a large Methodist church to play on their basketball team. Most of my life was conservative, playing cards and sports—a safe, sometimes interesting, but superficial life. But then my friends went off to college and I had to work. Later I had to go into the military. The heart of this book starts with this next phase of my life … in the Navy, Southern California, 1967, the *Summer of Love*.

Acknowledgments

This book could not have been created without the help of: Terry Winchester, Steve Kitzinger and Todd Yonts computer; Brittany Leary typing; my sister, Linda Young, typing, computer, and inspiration; and from iUniverse Molly O'Brian.

Introduction

This autobiography tells of the unique journeys (outward and inward) and the otherworldly visions of a '60s hippie, growing from the carefree communes and rock festivals into the timeless wisdom of the great mystics of our age.

Dyal takes us through his experiences with the gentle Buddhist Monk, Bhante Gunaratana.

Then we meet Baba Ram Dass, the American Yogi, previously known as Richard Alpert, who was fired from his teaching position at Harvard for working too closely with Timothy Leary on his LSD experiments.

Next we travel through California and Europe with Maharishi Mahesh Yogi, the early guru of the Beatles.

Then we're introduced to the American Yogi, Swami Rudrananda.

Pir Vilayat Khan, the Sufi (mysticism that includes all religions), takes us to a depth of reality few Americans even know exists.

We then travel to the Colorado mountain retreat of Swami Amar Jyoti.

Next we experience the power and incredible depth of insight of the Sikh master, Yogi Bhajan.

Chapter eleven is the Dalai Lama, Ocean of Wisdom, whose presence and techniques help us overcome our real enemies ... our inner afflictions.

In *Stray Visions and Insights* are experiences that don't fit into the other chapters, but are worth mentioning.

Then, we are enriched by a vision of the mythical Himalayan master, Babaji.

In the next chapter we learn of Sri Ganapati Sachchidananda Swamiji, the Great Master.

In the last chapter we hear of Karunamayi, the lady saint whose incarnation was foretold by the revered Ramana Maharshi.

PART I

Chapter One: Foolish Youth

In the summer of 1967, *The Summer of Love*, I was on active duty at the Naval Air Station in Los Alamitos, California.

One night, a friend and I were at our adjoining lockers, as we were preparing to go to the base movie.

He turns to me and says, "Here take this."

I reply, "What is it?"

"LSD."

"What's that?"

"Take it, you'll like it."

I took it, cautiously chewing a little.

"Swallow it!"

I swallowed. We turned and walked casually, towards the door, out the door, across the road, and some thirty yards down the dirt sidewalk.

At this point I was aware of a fluid shift in awareness. Instead of at my body looking out, I was inside the body, aware of all directions.

The body was perceived as a whole, completely fluid, yet the movements extended beyond. Though one with the environment, I limited my focus to just the body. No tension ... no boundaries ... just peace.

I was energized, yet calm. The night air was crisp and invigorating. A deep, strong breath entered from outside, circulated majestically through the entire system, then left in one continuous flow.

I was heavy, yet fluid. The body moved on its own, in flawless balance. I could feel the details of each muscle fiber, as it flexed in its turn of perfection.

My senses perceived the incredibly rich walk, as taking many hours, but my intellect knew it was only five minutes.

Once at the theater, there was a brief fear of how to continue. Yet the fear was short lived, as I was witness to an intellect functioning outside me. A ticket was purchased, words were spoken, refreshments procured, and the body smoothly settled in a good seat. I witnessed this all as a non-participating observer.

The movie, *Fantastic Voyage*, lasting an hour and a half, or so, was perceived by my senses to be five minutes.

I was intuitively drawn away from watching the movie, knowing there's a danger there.

Walking back to the barracks, I was much closer to my usual state. There was more control and reasoning, though life was still fluid.

Reflecting on this experience, there had been more fear than I'd acknowledged at the time. I read everything I could find on drugs.

I became interested in a new word, *hallucination*. My intellect couldn't understand how you could see something that wasn't there.

I read of early drug cultures—of the hashish club of intellectuals and artists, in nineteenth-century France. I decided to try it again.

A safe yet fantasy inducing place would seem to work best. Knott's Berry Farm seemed ideal.

I went to Knott's Berry Farm, took LSD, and walked around. Nothing seemed to happen early on. I began to enjoy the sights.

I was looking at an American West exhibit. There was a covered wagon behind restraining bars, a painted background of desert, plants, hills, and clouds. The clouds were majestically gliding across the sky. My intellect came in. This couldn't be happening? I was hallucinating!

I felt overly self-conscious. I looked around. No one was watching me—or were they? I had to move on to safer ground. Movement and a change of scene relaxed and energized me. I felt good. Colors were bright, like in a cartoon. Outlines were fluid, as all forms and colors flowed and changed.

I was standing next to a statue of a cowboy—or was it a real man? But it didn't move and looked too perfect to be real. I slowly reached to touch it. It moved! My hand jerked back. My heart beat faster. Did he see me? I turned and walked away, zigzagging through fields of moveable luminous statues. It was a long time before I could look back.

I tried to leave, to go where you could tell fantasy from reality, but I was traveling in circles.

There was a short line to an exhibit. Maybe inside there'd be less people. I could relax, get my bearings.

Big mistake! It was an exhibit of optical illusions. The guide was good. I was fascinated. He went too fast for my intellect to figure it all out. He proved to us that a short woman was taller than a very tall man. Gravity worked in different directions. I threw a ball a few feet into the air. It came down at a 45° angle, to one side. The guide began to play off of me, like I was a child. Maybe he thought I was kidding, or retarded. I became paranoid again, slithered into the background, and prayed for it all to be over. I became less high. Time went by slowly, but calmly, and then I was out. Walking around in the anonymous crowd was much better.

I made it to a telephone, called my girlfriend, and she came and rescued me.

I read more. Two particular ideas impressed me—first, the attitude of some American Indian tribes. The male, upon reaching his manhood age, would go off by himself for several days. He would take drugs and open up to his inner self. A *vision quest*, they called this. He wouldn't have taken any drugs before. His vision would show his place in the culture. It would actually come true—only in exceptional cases, or if he became a medicine man, would he take drugs again.

The second idea was from modern scientific research. In trying to understand how LSD and similar drugs work, scientists had postulated an intriguing theory. They believed that LSD was like a key that was close to the basic chemical structure that would activate electrical potential. Messages throughout our nervous system travel by chemical to electrical to chemical to electrical, ad infinitum. So this chemical key (LSD) causes a latent response in our nervous system to be activated. So what the drug reveals is our potential, though it is not exact, because it is prematurely activated. We are pushed further away from actually achieving our potential, because the system is weakened greatly by this premature stimulation.

At this time, I wound up with a different and better drug source. We had organic mescaline (from peyote) and organic psilocybin (from mushrooms). They produced less paranoia, less physical weakness, and more pleasant, subtle effects. Love and peace were activated. We no longer wanted the LSD and sometimes couldn't even find someone who'd take it.

I started smoking marijuana. My first time was riding on the freeway, listening to the car radio, the wonderful songs of 1967—depth, sensitivity, insights—opening a world of clarity and wonder. I was lifted to a place where reality was even greater than my dreams. The full, complete, wholeness of the music was like being in love. The music was crisp and clear, of depth and power, fluid and alive. It was, as if, this was the first time I had really *heard* music. Just to *feel*—the richness, the textures, the energy, and the subtleties—nothing else was needed or even thought of.

Usually I would just trip on the weekends, although not every weekend. I sometimes use the word trip for LSD, mescaline, or psilocybin, as I can't remember which one I used on each specific occasion.

I had a friend who knew Timothy Leary, the popular force behind the spread of LSD use. We even had LSD that Leary made. My friend also knew the members of the Grateful Dead. We'd go to a place we called The Barn (it was actually an old aircraft hangar) and see the Grateful Dead and Taj Mahal perform. We'd spend hours picking up people for each concert. On one occasion, one of the guys had to go on a blind date with one of his father's business associates. We found the girl's address, turned between two large white pillars, but still couldn't see the house. The house emerged as a huge white mansion with several limousines parked in front. Then we drove around the house and parked among the new sport cars. The children had a playhouse in the back that was furnished as well as most middle-class homes. An elaborate flower, tree, and herb garden separated by brick walkways stretched as far as the eye could see. Looking in the main house, through the glass wall and glass doors in the back, we could see a huge ballroom with the near left corner carpeted. The girl's father was sitting on a couch in work clothes watching TV. The girl was beautiful and nice, but only a favor for her date's father, as my friend's real girlfriend was then living in Paris. Finally at the concert sight, we smoked a joint while walking from the car, handed the joint to the security guard, who then took a hit and handed it back.

Once I went to my friend's apartment a little early, dropped acid, put the headphones on, and laid back to listen to the new Jefferson Airplane album. With my eyes closed, I could feel the music travel through my brain. Several hours later, I came out. There were people and food scattered all around. They told me that every now-and-then someone would get close to see if I was breathing, then go back to what they were doing.

I met the children of the ruling class. One guy was from a very wealthy family that held several prestigious positions. One couple was traveling, while friends of theirs were going to college under their names. Another guy was a world-class surfer, who spent has life searching for the best waves. Their parents rarely knew what they were doing, but would bail them out if needed, or even convince the law to go away. One told me that he only trusted the wealthy and the poor, for they were settled in their lot, while the ones in between were too conniving.

My job in the Navy was as a photographer. My older brother, Wayne, had told me that this was the best military job, and he was right. Once I met Dean Martin when he used our base for background on his Matt Helm movie, *The Ambushers*. He was an easy-going nice guy, just like he was in the movies and on TV. Once between scenes, he walked to the spectators and asked if anyone would like a photo with him. He then spent half an hour joking and posing with people. I still have photos from this event, including one of Dean and me.

Another time I got to go, as a photographer, to the opening of the Long Beach Navel Hospital. There I met Miss Indiana, and got a date to take her to Disneyland. On the way to pick her up my car broke down. I limped back to the base and tried to call her, but couldn't get through. It was late and she wasn't due to stay much longer, anyway. So, as far as she knows, I stood her up. I was very upset. Besides being beautiful, she seemed like a very sweet girl. Little twists of fate, like this, can be so significant.

I learned to juggle from one of the other trippers on the base. I was too tense to learn straight, but picked it up quickly when stoned. It got to be that if you juggled you were suspected of doing drugs, so, you couldn't juggle with any officers looking. When stoned, some movements left a visible trail. We called these *tracers*. Juggling tracers were particularly mesmerizing.

I had heard that Tina Turner practiced her show with the whole band and back-up singers at a nearby bar. This seemed too good to be true, as I was a fan of hers, and had yet to see her in person. I found the bar—it was all true. I would drink enough to be able to dance in public. The drinking plus the drugs loosened me up enough to where, eventually, I could even do well in dance contests, finding the dancing cathartic.

I took a night class in Classical Music. Another student and I would hide behind the bushes and smoke pot during the break. We seemed to enjoy the second half more than anyone else.

Usually tripping followed a general pattern. It would build for about an hour, peak for another four hours, then taper off for four more. So, if I started tripping after work, I would be back to normal by the next morning—but once the drug took effect much slower, so that when I had to go to work I was still peaking. Colors were bright and fluid, so intensely distracting that I was incapable of focusing on normal conversation. My boss talked for what seemed like a very long time—telling me what I had to do for that day. I was to delegate this work to some twenty-five others. Not knowing what he said, I had to guess. Once caught being wrong, I lied my way out of it, by saying we were out of a needed material. Needless to say, I never tripped again when I had to work the next day.

There I met my first real girlfriend, Patti Banta. First time I saw her was when I walked into my off-base apartment. She was there singing with her Christian folk singing group. They were actually very talented and creative. One of my roommates was working with Christian missionaries that were connected to her group. She was exceptional musically, intellectually, and even ran fast enough to be considered an Olympic hopeful. At the time I was a forward on one of the best military basketball teams. Once we were out walking, but ran into rush hour traffic on a large road. I grabbed her hand while looking for an opening—quickly started running as I finally spotted one. When on the other side, I had expected to be pulling her, but she was ahead of me. Then she confessed her running ability. She had so many abilities that could intimidate the boys, so she tried to hide some of them.

She only tripped once. Saying good night to her on that date, I visually saw her melt, though I knew it didn't really happen. We went to one rock festival. She felt it was too crowded. We saw the movie *2001: A Space Odyssey* on Sunset Boulevard. I was tripping, so the movie in my head was even more other-worldly. She remembered where the car was, but I had a driving problem. I couldn't tell what color the light was. Besides the red, green, and yellow, I saw other colors, all of which were continuously changing. So, I had to turn right for a long time, until I was down enough to see the real colors.

Another time I was too high to drive, so I turned into a side street to parallel park. The next car passing me honked furiously. Looking around, I noticed I was going the wrong way on a one way street, so pulled into a parking lot, parked, and walked home.

Yet another time, I started getting paranoid, so pulled into a crowded parking lot. Just standing there was worse, so I walked into a small convenience store. Looking at the luminous items in the store, I noticed the clerk staring at me, so went to the counter to buy something. On the counter was a small magazine with a front page drawing of Revolutionary War marchers—one marcher carrying a flag, one playing a flute, and one hobbling in a leg caste. I saw the colorful marchers, march out of the magazine, and slowly continue across the counter. Realizing the clerk couldn't see this, I quickly paid for my items and left. I still had to walk around the parking lot, long enough for enough cars to leave, so I could tell which one was mine.

Developing organically within the new drug culture was something we called a *trip guide*. Meaning it was usually necessary to have someone with you your first time. One of Patti's friends wanted to trip. Some of us got together to discuss it. It was unanimous—she wasn't ready. She didn't even handle ordinary reality well.

Once when I had weekend duty Patti was with another man. She told me as we were driving home late one night. I was thrown, as I didn't even consider this a possibility. I saw a semi in front of us, drove beside it to pass, then looked towards it … it wasn't there! Then I noticed I was going eighty in a thirty zone, so calmed down, and slowed down. After many phone calls we made up.

For a short time I had a third shift job as a security guard. Driving back to the base in the crisp morning air, I'd listen to a radio station that played one side of a Bob Dylan album and one side of a Jimmy Hendrix album. This high often felt even better than my drug trips.

Another job while I was still in California, but just out of the military, was as an assistant manager in a pizza parlor. We had a great jukebox that would get me high even when I wasn't on drugs. Every employee did drugs, but since I still had short hair, one of the narc, wannabe customers confided in me. While I was stoned, I'd lie to him about the others. One day I opened the store but was still hallucinating. I had to guess which of the soft drinks were which, and completely forgot about one of the customers. When the manager came in, I had to tell him that I was too high to work. He said that he was also, so we had to close the business.

A few months after leaving California I was going to Indiana University in Bloomington, Indiana. My California experiences helped me fit into the drug culture at IU. Again, I lucked into a more educated environment. We centered on a woman with two little girls. Her ex-husband was a college professor. Sometimes the little girls would save questions for me from drawings in college science books. Reading the surrounding text I was barely capable of explaining it on their level. We never tripped when the girls were around.

Only once did I come to the apartment when she was the only one there. We decided to go out. While she was bathing, a short man with a lot of hair came to the door. I told him the situation, and as he left he said, "Do I have to worry about you?" She told me later that he was a local musician and very talented.

I remember *seeing* the music come out of the stereo.

One day I heard that the musical *Hair* was playing that night in Indianapolis. I looked quickly for my party friends, but couldn't find them. As this could be a once-in-a-lifetime opportunity, I hitchhiked to Indy. It was great. I was even close enough to dance on the stage with the performers when the show was winding down. A few days later, my friends told me they were in the cheap seats, and very surprised to see me dancing on the stage.

Two of the girls I partied with moved out of their dorm into a small house with another girl. Celebrating with them, we wound up still tripping the next morning while watching Saturday cartoons. I'm sitting in a lounge chair in front of the TV, unsure where the cartoons end and my hallucinations begin. Safe among friends, as the outer world is tenuous at best. The new girl comes and sits on the floor in front of me, leaning against my chair. She's wearing a large robe. I see her drop the robe revealing an exquisite nude form. My mind is telling me this can't be real, so I go back to watching the cartoons. The next day the girls tell me it was real, but that was my only chance.

They woke me up late one night to go to the supermarket. They were too high and needed a straight person to do the shopping. Relaxing with them in the supermarket, I was getting a *contact high*, so they felt that I'm the one that has to be watched.

One night we were tripping, as some were straightening a white powder on a table. I hadn't done this before, or even since. They called me over, telling me to go first, and handed me a straw. They falsely assumed I knew what was going on. I guessed that with one end of the straw in my nose I should inhale the powder. I quickly inhaled the whole line, then was angrily told it was divided into individual sections. Shortly my heart began to beat irregularly, and breathing was strained. Frightened, I called my girlfriend, Kathie, but by the time she arrived I was back to normal. She was a very sweet girl, but I was too immature to appreciate her. She didn't do drugs. We'd calmly drink tea and listen to Moody Blues in her apartment. She had a big heart and a little rabbit, and was kinder to me than I deserved.

The next summer I worked in a pizza parlor in Bloomington. School was close to starting again, so the employees had a party. These were people I didn't know well. I was already tripping when I arrived. Some people were drunk. There was a crying baby in a side room, which no one was attending. Not a pleasant environment, so I left to walk in the cool night air. Tension dissolved, as I became strong and fluid. Clearly, I felt my father's presence inside me. I could feel that in the little conservative town where he was raised, one drink made him an alcoholic and one fight made him a bully—that I had chosen this life to get has raw power as fuel, with the blessing of him leaving, taking the misuse of that energy with him.

Back in my home town of Evansville, Indiana, an old friend introduced me as a real hippie. My hair was now longer than most men in this area. An elderly couple ran their car over the sidewalk trying to hit me. I was invited to a party at the home of the local head shop owner. I had two hits left, took one and gave one to him. He split his four ways and gave three of the sections to his friends. I took my hit, mingled with the others, enjoying the fresh air in the isolated log home in dense woodland. The other trippers sat motionless for hours. Afterwards one of them asked me how I could move.

After this I mainly did pot, and not even much of that. The brother of a girl I liked kept trying to get me to try some of his drugs. Once he said he had the best acid to ever be in Evansville. I agreed to take one, just to shut him up. It was so weak it would have taken a hundred hits to equal one California hit. A similar thing happened with some University of Evansville students, with the same result.

I ran into a friend from high school who was now an expert pot grower. Every six months, or so, I'd get stoned with him and go on a vision quest. I'd only do it when I felt stuck. I'd also do Tai Chi and meditate—every time an answer would come. Usually it was that I was pushing-the-river, not going with life's flow—except once when it was the opposite—I wasn't doing enough. Eventually I lost contact with him, but I had already discovered that Yoga was a much better vision quest.

At the end of three straight days of partying, I was at a home where a pizza was delivered. My job was to put the slices in individual plates. Only part of the pizza was on the table, with the rest leaning over the side. I put a few of the pieces resting on the table into individual plates. Then the rest of the pizza flipped onto the floor. This jolted me awake, for clearly I had partied too long. I left immediately.

The last time I tripped was in the apartment of a friend of my girlfriend. I had been doing Yoga for several years. This trip was partly to see what control I could have within the trip, utilizing my budding mental control. There was a large photo on one wall. I started imagining it was real ... the room disappeared, as all I could see was the photo, and it became three dimensional. Wanting to utilize this new consciousness I went into a side room to meditate. Working my way up the body's psychic centers, I was feeling more consciousness shifts, but having to fight against limited self control. Then my girlfriend came in. She was on her first trip. It was difficult to convince her that I couldn't have sex at that time, because I didn't have a body. She finally left, but my meditation was ruined.

I lived, for a short while, with some old hippies, in the college town of Ann Arbor, Michigan. They had evolved various kinds of co-ops and even some successful regular businesses. At a party with around sixty people, five were drinking alcohol and five were smoking pot. Most were just talking and dancing. This is what we've evolved into. Vision Quests have grown into actual manifestations.

My experience with non-organic drugs, or super concentrated drugs like heroin and cocaine, were minimal and unpleasant. Their physical drain was greater. There vision potential was practically nil, so there was no reason to even take them once. Death could result from even once. An all-too-vivid example of this is Len Bias, who was a basketball star at Maryland and top draft pick of the Boston Celtics. This also illustrates that drugs can actually be more harmful to healthy people, as a healthy person has already released some of his adrenaline, naturally. The increased adrenaline release from drug use, can be too much; thus death, (e.g., Len Bias).

One episode of the *Oprah*, TV show, showed autopsies on young people who had died from meth use. Their brains were eaten away like an elderly person's with Alzheimer's. Horrible stuff—there is no reason to do meth even once.

I became sure that Yoga exercises gave clearer insights, and without any side effects.

Even if drugs were harmless, the fact that they're illegal would be sufficient reason for not doing them. The tangible threat of going to jail, and the social paranoia accompanying drug use, both hurt the quality of one's life.

The dangerous or stupid people, one may encounter in the drug culture, are definitely worth avoiding. Also, these days, it's difficult to know what you're really getting.

Although there are some reasonable medical uses for some drugs, particularly marijuana, the legalization would cause too much harm. Smoke affects people close enough, in distance and time, to breathe the same air. Marijuana relaxes the spine and activates brain cells; but with the end result that the spine is weakened and brain cells are destroyed, as Yogi Bhajan has stated. It follows, as I have also noticed, that it is particularly harmful to children. Smoking Calamus Root with pot neutralizes some of the negative effects.

Chapter Two: Communes

My military service ended. Patti and I married, and I started in college.

I was going to school on the G.I. Bill. It was several months behind, so I got a job in a pizza parlor. I'd go to school, go to work, and then try to study. I was so tired, I'd take coffee and No-Doz to try and stay awake—but I'd shortly fall asleep, anyway.

I had a nervous breakdown, left everything in California, and went back to Indiana. After several months I regained some composure, and decided to return to California to see if I still had a wife—we'd never really had a fight.

Hitchhiking just west of St. Louis, in the summer of 1969, two semis stop, they're traveling from Chicago to L.A. with large statues and signs that are used for motion picture publicity. There's plenty of room, but it's very hot inside.

They pick up every hitchhiker. By the time we reach the Grand Canyon there are about twenty-five of us.

I had never seen the Grand Canyon. We arrive just before sunrise. We sit, waiting. One guy begins playing his guitar. He's very good. The sunrise begins. A gigantic canyon majestically, slowly, unfolds before us. The guitar player describes the expanding scenes—where he's been, where no one's been, where the animals are.

The guitar player says his name is John Deutschendorf. He's going to concentrate on his solo career, and change his name to one that's easier to remember … John Denver.

John, a tall guy named Clint who's heading for San Francisco, and myself, camp out on a large hill that has only dirt paths and small bushes. The next morning we hitchhike our separate ways.

I fail at getting my wife back. The marriage mainly failed because of my immaturity. I still use our love as a touchstone for romantic relationships. Many years later, after we both had other marriages, we reconnected. I write, e-mail, and sometimes talk to her on the phone. There can be only one first love. I hope to see her again someday.

I wind up identifying with the song, *Leaving on a Jet Plane.* It's the sad breakup of my marriage; yet the joy of having been loved, and then the freedom of being single and carefree. My mother also relates that song to my failed marriage. A chill is sent through my spine, many years later, when I realize my hitchhiking buddy, John, actually wrote the song.

It's too unpleasant to stay in California, so I leave. I'm going towards Indiana, but with no real destination, some money hidden in my socks, an invigorating sense of freedom, though there are still moments of sadness.

I meet other hitchhikers, interesting and good people.

I hitchhike some with an engineer from England. He works one year and travels for four. He's either going to a commune in New Mexico or to Florida to get a tan. He decides to go to Florida. I decide to go to the commune. It's close. He says there are good people there.

I go north of Albuquerque, right on a dirt road to Placitas. There are poor adobe homes, built close together. There's little sign of life, only hills and scrub brush, dust and sun. I'm told the commune I want is further down the road.

I find, off the road, a huge geodesic dome. There are a few people living in a small section against the wall. They tell me there use to be a lot of people here, but the commune I want is across the road towards Placitas.

Walking back, I see a few mailboxes—this must be it.

I follow a dirt path down some hundred yards. Adobes start appearing. A couple of shadowy figures walk into one. I decide to go to this one.

The door is open. I walk in. There are cots on both sides, a window on the right wall. Against the far wall, stretches large solid wooden bunk beds, large enough for eight people. Clothes and ordinary personal belongings are stuffed under the beds and in corners.

I hear soft conversation coming from a doorway to the left. I walk up to the doorway. Inside is a dirty old couch and easy chair, a couple of plain wooden chairs, a fireplace, and a woodbox full of wood.

I'm thinking, "This place could be too unhealthy to live in."

A dirty man about thirty, with a long beard, too many clothes on, and deep dark eyes, says to me, "You don't have to stay if you don't want to!"

I say nothing.

I later learn this is Crazy Bill. He was one of the first hippies, was beaten up often. He rarely leaves this room, says he astral travels to visit old friends.

I wind up living in this building for two months. There are about nine adobes, with a total of about fifty people. My adobe has from six to twelve people. Years later, I read we were called the *Lower Farm*, but while there I never heard that name.

Everyone is interesting, has some unique strength, with the predominate attitude of caring, relaxing, and helping.

I dig an underground home with a couple from California. She's physically beautiful but gets mad if you mention it. The work is hard, but we only work when we want to.

My body is getting healthier and my mind clearer; even though, often, all we have to eat are white flour tortillas. One really needs so little to be happy. Good friends mean so much. With the pressure off, I see what really matters.

There was one couple that had a little girl of five. She was protected, but not lied to, or told she had limits. Once she was drawing on a table in my adobe. She was drawing different people as lines—nicer people were wavy lines, troubled people jagged lines. I usually could tell who she was drawing. The exception was a man I saw as more jagged. I tried to see him through her eyes; and from then on, I understood him better.

A Mexican, who spoke little English, was there. I didn't speak Spanish, but somehow, sometimes, I knew what he wanted to say, and would interpret for him.

There were broken hearts, broken dreams, but most people simply found this a better life. One man, who had lived in other communes, said this one was the best, because we had no specific agenda to push.

Another man in the commune was called Speed. He was short, muscular, and in his mid-twenties. He drew wonderful murals. He was the best mechanic, but hid it, because others would overload him with work requests. Speed had been in Vietnam. He was handed a medal in an elaborate ceremony; but refused to accept, because they didn't even mention his buddy, who died next to him. Speed was arrested, and then forgiven, because he's a hero. He just left, couldn't deal with the hypocrisy.

There were some, over ripe, jimson weed plants growing nearby. I'd never tried that drug. Getting drugs directly from nature seems to be a weakness of mine. They told me three would kill you, but they were old, so I ate five.

I went back to my adobe. One of the few times, pot was available. I smoked some, and then felt the need for fresh air.

I walked the side path, through the shrubs and small trees. I saw the tree roots, turn into moving snakes, with open mouths. The bushes turned into animal bodies, with huge mouths. I tried to step over and around them, but they were growing in number and speed. Their colors were becoming more varied and luminous. I realized I was lost—turned around, to see I'd only gone twenty yards, and then easily walked back to safety.

A couple of the guys, hitchhiking back to the commune, brought with them the men who had picked them up. One was a nice fellow who played guitar. The other was a brainwashed Christian, who brought us some wine, and then tried to convert us. Most of us didn't want any alcohol in the commune. The Christian got drunk, and then wanted to fight. We made him leave. That was the only really negative encounter, while I was there.

There was a van full of people from the East Coast that stayed about a week. Their leader was an old guy, who had taken a lot of drugs, and was given early retirement from his government job. They were going to Mexico. One of their ladies stayed with me.

There were two books in the commune. The one I read was *The Master Game,* by Dr. De Ropp.

Dr. De Ropp believes that we all play games. Usually the goal is power, wealth, lust, or something else that's ego related—or, The Master Game, the game to reach the ultimate.

The first step is to have a healthy body, because unless we have a healthy body our perceptions aren't accurate. The best way to get a healthy body is through Yoga (Hatha Yoga, the physical Yoga). This systematically progresses into deeper levels of mental concentration, until we merge with our infinite, limitless, joyful soul. This was the first time I'd heard of Yoga.

I stayed in other communes, in Virginia, Missouri, Tennessee, Michigan, and Indiana. Some were based on the book *Walden Two* by Behavioral Psychologist B. F. Skinner. This book had an ideal society with a fair system of labor distribution called *labor-credits*, with an equal sharing of profits, and whatever else could reasonably be shared. In application it had great merit, with a major drawback of being overly intellectual; thus being able to rationalize behavior that more perceptive people would know to be wrong.

Another commune was larger and more successful. I decided I was going to try and get a girlfriend with a big heart—not obsess on the superficial. One girl stood out. We became lovers. Still considered a visitor, but because of my relationship with her, I knew some of the commune secrets—even knew the hiding place of the secret discussions. Late one night I read them to see what was said of me, then spoke of them to my friends. Only one writing was negative. They told me to ignore it, as the writer was always negative, and they wanted to get rid of her, but because she was one of the first members, it was difficult to do.

I had overheard mention of a specific location. Its name had a poetic lilt to it, though I didn't know what was there. On a rare day off, looking for something to do, I noticed a section of the commune map that could fit the mystery description, so decided to walk there. After a short distance through the woods a path emerged. Reaching the described spot, I saw a commune member sitting on a log, just outside the commune's boundary. As he also saw me, I had to walk up to him in a non-threatening manner. He handed me a joint and said, "When you're through, just put it in the log." I smoked a little, put the rest in the log, and then walked back.

We tried to play non-competitive games, but the athletes among us would stay after for more intense competition. Some didn't understand this, but it seemed natural to me.

We were top heavy on the intellectual side with four Electrical

Engineers out of some sixty people, but the most valuable was a man who could fix the cars.

My next commune was connected to the last one, so I was accepted immediately. It was more isolated, with a more laid back attitude. I was invited to come there by a guy who said I'd like it more. There was a stream that touched the property. We'd go skinny dipping. At first I thought I'd get an ulcer from trying not to stare at the shapely ladies, but eventually I got use to it. Once I was in the water as a water moccasin swam a few feet from me. One guy told me the snake wouldn't hurt me, but I didn't go in the water again.

Traveling to an even larger commune with a gypsy-like, lady friend, Kim, we picked up a hitchhiker. The hitchhiker was a regular of the commune. She had a small ornate box in which she kept what she called her power objects—I could feel energy coming from the box. She said she'd been in Cuba and had an affair with Castro, and that our government was always following her. Just inside the commune at the gatehouse, a large limousine pulls in behind us, turns around and leaves. Its license plate says US Government.

We're assigned a trailer that three others are already in. One guy is a bit creepy so I sleep close to my friend, even though she says it isn't necessary. I have a dream that the creepy guy tries to force himself on her, and I make a grumbling noise like I'm waking up, which makes him leave. The next day I mention this to her, and she tells me that it actually happened. The vast majority of people that live in communes are good people.

I next go to a smaller, less structured commune. We have four goats. I'm the only one that likes to get up early, so I do the early morning milking. A young runaway stays with us briefly. He writes frightening poetry. When he comes into a room all the ladies leave. Two men from Germany stayed briefly.

It seemed to me, clearly, that the best and only fulfilling life, would be to have both this natural communal life and the Yogic knowledge—the Yogic knowledge to deepen and stabilize the communal life; and the communal life to manifest, express, and fulfill the deeper knowledge of our nature inherent in Yoga.

I left to find this Yogic knowledge, and then to return to communal life.

Chapter Three: Rock Festivals

While in California in the '60s, my future wife and I went to a rock festival. There were some fifty thousand people there. We sat unobtrusively among the masses. Occasionally a joint would be handed to us; we'd take a hit and pass it on. Then a flask of wine, we'd take a drink and pass it on. I liked the sharing. She didn't like the cramped spaces.

I came back alone the next day. This time I was tripping. Shortly after paying and walking inside, a cop ran towards me, pointing and shouting, "There's one!" I immediately turned and ran. After running a long distance, I stopped and looked behind me. I'd escaped. I found out later some people had climbed over a fence without paying. The cop must have thought I was one of the fence jumpers.

This time, I went closer to the stage. I found an open area, and allowed the music and drugs to move me in dance—very cathartic.

My dancing space got too small to freely flow in. I could see the crowd pushing in on me. I had difficulty breathing. I hurried out, stepping clumsily, around and between, the seated audience. One person looked at me, as I passed, and said in an incredulous tone, "Look at him!"

Further from the stage, there was more air, and room to move in. You could meet, relate, and enjoy. Most of the time, there was peace and harmony.

Another Rock Festival, several years later in Southern Illinois, was more enjoyable. I went with a friend, whose father was a private detective. We set up tents next to each other, and I don't see him again, 'till weeks later.

Still at the Illinois Festival, casually walking around, I noticed a policeman. Walking straight towards him, was a very young girl, with vacant eyes. She was obviously too stoned to know what she was doing. I walked between them, turned facing her and told her, "There's a cop there, he'll bust you!" She couldn't speak. She followed me around for several hours, like a small child away from home for the first time. I got her something to eat and drink. We ran into a small group about her age, with the same blank stares. She walked up to them. No words were spoken. They walked off together. She didn't look back. I never saw her again.

Walking around, I happened to be close to some people that were sharing a huge marijuana pipe. They passed it on to me. I took my turn, and then passed it on. I noticed this expensive camper trailer a few feet away. A very attractive girl started talking to me. She looked like a college cheerleader. We smoked together. We went for a walk. We took our clothes off and bathed in the open-air showers. We sat in her car. I loaned her my shirt. We talked. When she found out the trailer wasn't mine, her tone changed. She got out of the car and walked away. I was too stoned to be upset, just a surrealistic lesson. I never saw her again.

I meet two girls from the East Coast. They had a large dog and a coatimundi. The coatimundi was from South America and looked like a raccoon. It'd search your pockets with its pointed head. We (humans and animals) were like a family. I gave the girls money to get us some food. I watched the animals while they were gone. The dog got in a vicious, snarling confrontation with another dog. I told him in a firm voice to, "Stop it!" He quit immediately, and walked away from the other dog. That was a clear, strong, feeling of attunement, like I had stumbled on a new scientific discovery. The dog had only known me for half an hour, yet he knew to mind me, and I knew to instruct him.

I was one of the people there that would run and slide in the mud. A year, or so, after this rock festival, I was in a park in Indianapolis. There I also slid in the mud. Then I stood up, and saw sliding by me a guy who had done the same at the Illinois festival. He may have recognized me too, but we never spoke.

The most interesting rock festival was the *Celebration of Life Music Festival in New Orleans* in June, 1971. I was traveling with a lady schoolteacher, on her summer vacation.

We met some locals who were students at LSU, and traveled with them, in and out of the festival. They were followers of *Babaji*. They taught us the chant: *Om Kriya Babaji Namah Om.* They were taught that the only rule for their relationship was that they could not say or do anything that would give the other doubts—this felt very wise to me.

The festival had a hill where those into metaphysics stayed. I'm walking on that hill. In the distance is a group walking towards me. As we approach each other, I see some of them have turbans on. In the front is a powerful looking man. The others are spread behind him, like birds flying behind their leader. At this point, in my life, I'm interested in Yoga, but still taking drugs. My direction has no clear vision or discipline. I stop. They continue walking past me. I'm looking, open to learning. The leader looks at me, straight in the eye, just a second's glance. The glance clearly gives me the message that my indecisive state limits my worthiness to only a second of his time.

I later heard this Yogi's name was Yogi Bhajan.

I felt the turmoil I thought Yogi Bhajan had seen, was from my indecision on where drugs fit with Yoga. I decided to take some Mescaline, go back to the hill, and see if some of my turmoil could be cleared.

The next day I took the mescaline and returned to the festival. The drug had taken effect. My body felt light and strong. I was relaxed and clear. What I saw was actually there, although the colors were more vivid and the outlines more distinct, like in a cartoon.

Walking up the hill, I see the turbaned people sitting under a large tent, I sit among the congregation. The leader sings this phrase, which I believe is "Why Guru." The others repeat it. The whole scene is very relaxing, energizing, and uplifting. I start saying "Why Guru" with the congregation. Once I just think it, and instantaneously I transcend. I drop inside myself, deeper than the body, deeper than tension—very pleasing and freeing. At this exact moment, a turbaned lady sitting in front of me turns and smiles, looking directly in my eyes. Could she feel me transcend?

The gathering casually moves outside the tent. I notice clouds overhead. There's a round hole in the clouds. Wherever Yogi Bhajan moves the hole follows him. At this time, this doesn't seem extraordinary. It's like a simple self-evident truth. Years later, I read where Yogi Bhajan said he had the water Siddhi (control over the element of water).

I'm walking towards Yogi Bhajan. There's heat and pressure. It increases the closer I get. At about six feet it's physically impossible to move closer. What's happening? I looked around. There's a circle of people around him—no one closer than six feet. I watch.

People approach with questions and gifts. Two of the gifts are: a painting and a song. One lady is rebuffed for a subtle sexual gesture. Yogi Bhajan is the freest man I've ever seen. He's alive to the subtle, the powerful, and the energy of the present. He's beyond rules or limits, yet he is the embodiment of discipline, the discipline that comes from nature, not that imposed by the limits of the human intellect.

People come with their question of the moment—are given the answer—leave with an answer that they can't wisely fit, to the next moment. If two are given the same answer, a safe and comforting rule springs up. Yogi Bhajan remains ever free and alive, even untouched by his own wisdom.

Years later, reflecting on my experiences, I had a startling realization. The feeling from the seemingly opposite applications of discipline, of Yoga and anarchical communal life, was the same. Reflecting further, I realized that these two extremes had in common that they were based on reality. Yoga is the deepest knowledge, given to us by our most perceptive souls. Communal life, when the tension is off and spontaneity and honest are valued, tends to be based on our truest nature. Everything in between is based to some degree on conceptions superimposed on reality. We are trying to deform reality to mold it into our concepts rather than looking directly at life.

PART II

Chapter Four: Bhante Gunaratana, the Buddhist Monk

Several years later, I went to a meditation retreat. It was lead by a Buddhist Monk from Sri Lanka, Bhante Gunaratana. The meditation he taught was called Vipassana or Insight Meditation.

I mention Bhante before the other teachers, because his techniques provide a very solid and reasonable foundation.

The retreat was on a small hill on a farm in Southern Indiana. The couple that owned the farm also made pottery.

Bhante was small, robed, and shaven headed. His English was very good, but more impressive was his serene speaking tone, which relaxed and enlivened you, even when you couldn't follow his meaning.

The more you were around him, the wiser he became, yet his personality was that of a simple, good person, unimposing, and clear.

The meditation was to sit, with eyes closed, and watch the breath, watch inhale, and watch exhale. Any thoughts, other body sensations, or emotions, were to be treated indifferently, like they were someone walking past you on a sidewalk. You notice they're there, and then drop them from your focus, and continue on your way. If you need to, you adapt a simple counting of breaths; or think the word inhale, as you inhale, and think the word exhale, as you exhale.

This is alternated with a walking meditation. In the walking meditation, the point of focus is the six moments of the feet as you walk. The six moments are: the heel lifts from the floor, toes lift from the floor, the foot moves through the air, the heel touches the floor, the toes touch the floor, and the foot balances. The walk is slow and deliberate, with the feet shoulder width apart, and each step about that distance. If this becomes easy, then awareness of the breath is brought in. Any tension is relaxed. The gaze is on the floor, about ten feet in front of you.

These meditations relax and clear the mind, give you the ability to see what's actually there. Buddhists believe it best to bring in as little as possible; because to have a clear mind, you'll have to eventually drop your aids, anyway. There is much merit in this. At least, it's a good foundation, to limit your entanglement in the complications and addictions that often occur along the way.

During breaks in the meditation session we ate, socialized, and played games. During one break, I taught Bhante to throw a Frisbee. Later, I taught him to throw a controlled curve. Within a few minutes we were throwing to each other around the corner of the farmhouse, sight unseen.

The farmhouse had a large bathroom, next to the dining room. The bathroom had comfortable chairs, and was thus a relaxing place to talk. Late one night, several ladies were in there talking, with the door open. I was sitting in the dining room. Bhante walked up to the bathroom door. Upon hearing the ladies talking, he stopped and just stood there.

I walked up to Bhante and politely informed him that the ladies were just talking, and would simply leave if asked. Bhante seemed uneasy. I volunteered to ask the ladies to leave. Bhante said nothing. I went and informed the ladies that Bhante wanted in the restroom. They left immediately, but Bhante was gone. I sat in the dining room for about half an hour, and didn't see him return.

The meditation sessions were in the loft of a large barn. We would alternate sitting and walking meditations. This felt very natural. After sitting you felt like walking, and after walking, you felt like sitting.

At the end of one sitting meditation, I spaced out … then suddenly was awake, as if I had just been startled awake, from a deep sleep. Yet I was calm, centered, there were no thoughts, no body feeling at all. My eyes were closed. I heard some voices, faint, far off, down a tunnel that stretched in front of me. A little concern came to me. What was going on? Where was I? I focused on the voices. They became clearer, closer, louder. Body awareness came back. I slowly opened my eyes. I was sitting with five or six people in a small circle. When the meditation started, there were about twenty-five of us, sitting randomly. I felt centered, relaxed, and strong.

Once, I was privileged to accompany Bhante on a short trip to speak to some children. It was a beautiful day. Bhante spoke on a grassy hill beside some shade trees. He told simple stories of the Buddha. There was a feeling of pervasive perfection. This was much better than the grown-up talks.

I saw Bhante a few times in Evansville. One time I took a city bus, and then walked a few miles to the home where Bhante would speak. After sitting there a few minutes, my mother walked in. I was surprised and delighted. Early on, she was my only relative interested in my metaphysical studies. We both found Bhante's talk inspiring. We left together in a cab.

In later years, I found the sitting meditation worked best, for me, if I also became aware of the held breaths (both before and after inhalation)—still with no regulation, just watching. I found I didn't need the counting techniques, and they were even a handicap. I also discovered that if I felt any tension it worked best if I relaxed the tension immediately. This is really an undoing, not a doing.

Bhante published an interesting autobiography in 2003.

Chapter Five: Baba Ram Dass, the American Trailblazer

When Timothy Leary was doing his famous LSD experiments at Harvard, he was kicked out in 1963 with another professor, Richard Alpert. Whereas Leary stayed with drugs, Alpert grew into mysticism. Alpert meet genuine Yoga masters. His name was changed to Baba Ram Dass (servant of God).

Baba Ram Dass wrote successful books, most notably *Be Here Now*, lectured, practiced, and helped spread understanding of Yoga. Yoga means union, union of your lesser and higher self, or, depending on your reference point, union with nature, or union with God. Yoga is that technical know-how.

I mention Baba Ram Dass here as much for his honesty as for his accomplishments. If anyone is truthful to himself and others, he is an asset in the growth of the spiritual, no matter what level of accomplishment. It is only those that deceive that cause harm.

Once we have chosen our path, comparison to other paths only dilutes our energy for growth, and shows our real lack of commitment. The means of transportation is not as important as actually reaching the goal. A sign of our growth is that when we touch our own Spirit we come to see that same Spirit in all others.

I was living in Evansville and heard that Baba Ram Dass was going to be in Bloomington, Indiana, for the weekend. Some friends and I crammed into a Volkswagen and drove to Bloomington. It wasn't until we arrived, that I heard that the man who invited us was Ram Dass's sponsor. We would be staying in the same house with Ram Dass.

I had visited the house, briefly, years earlier, when it was a Hari Krishna Ashram. An ashram is a place where one or more people live and work at spiritual growth.

We entered through a side door into a large kitchen, alive with the aromas of herbs, flowers, fruits, and coffee. I walked out the front door, to get out of the way, and stretch in the fresh air. I leaned against the cement railing that surrounds the spacious porch. I'm facing the door.

To my left is a couple sitting on a wooden bench, against the house. We're under shade, and there's a soft cool breeze.

Then a bearded, long-haired man in Americanized Indian clothing appears in the doorway. I know it's Ram Dass. We're facing each other. A casual glance, then my awareness lightly flows, through his eyes, and down the spine to his heart. At the heart, I clearly feel my own reflection. The glance is over. I'm back to normal perception.

Ram Dass walks to the bench. He sits down. I casually walk over and sit facing him. No one speaks for several minutes. The weather is perfect. We're shaded from the heat. The cool breeze still caresses. There is no traffic, only nature's noises. Ram Dass begins to softly chant. We politely join in. The four of us chant for what seems several hours. Some people come. Ram Dass get up and leaves. It's time to go to his lecture.

The lecture hall is filled to capacity, about five thousand. The talk is mainly on concepts I've heard before. The audience is quiet, respectful, and attentive.

After speaking for over an hour, Ram Dass starts chanting. Most people join in. The air becomes thick and alive. My body is light, strong, and fluid. The chanting's magical, blissful waves wash away all worldly cares. After about half an hour, it's time to leave the auditorium. We all stand. The chanting never stops. We slowly, orderly, leave the building. The chanting continues. Outside, we slowly shift locations. Many stay. The chanting doesn't seem to diminish. Finally Ram Dass says it's time to disperse for the night. We go our separate ways.

Back at the house, there were some fifty of us scrunched into the living room. Ram Dass sat in a lounge chair against one wall. The rest of us sat on the floor, facing him.

There's no set format. Organizers are in and out, with plans and details, then some calm. Ram Dass occasionally says that this has to be short. All of us want to stay there all night, but no one applies any pressure.

Now everyone's sitting—a few questions to Ram Dass—he speaks. One of his stories was of a little girl, a sweet child with an incurable disease. Ram Dass was working with her family, to ease their pain, but he became so attached to the child that when she died he also was overcome with grief. Several months later, Ram Dass was with his Guru, Neem Karoli Baba, who's affectionately referred to as Maharajji. Maharajji asked him how he liked meeting the lady saint. Ram Dass replied that he didn't know what he meant, as he had not seen a lady saint lately. Maharajji explained that the little girl was a high soul who had chosen that body, because for the work she was doing, she didn't need to stay long.

Ram Dass interpreted this as a lesson that his emotional response was from lack of knowledge, and that being off center is never good.

He said he didn't see Timothy Leary anymore, that they didn't have any more mutual Karma to work on.

Ram Dass spoke of the time he took LSD to Maharajji. He was curious about how Maharajji would react to the drug. Ram Dass held out a hand full of LSD. His expectation was that Maharajji would take one hit, but before he could explain, Maharajji took the whole handful and swallowed them quickly. Ram Dass was stunned, and waited impatiently. It didn't seem to affect the Guru. Later, at the appropriate time, Maharajji stated that the drug had an effect something like Samadhi.

Ram Dass spoke of the traps and joys of his journey. He was honest about his mistakes and the things that he was still working on. The overall effect was an opening of the heart, and a strengthening of belief in the spiritual path.

Chapter Six: Maharishi Mahesh Yogi, the Popular Yogi

In the spring of 1971, I went to Indianapolis to get initiated into Transcendental Meditation (TM). There was a beautiful Sanskrit ritual with flowers and incense. Then I was given my individualized mantra (sound used for the vibratory effect) to meditate on. My initiator was Bill Gates. The last I heard of him, he was going to build a boat and travel around the world.

I didn't feel any effects until weeks later in Evansville. Several times my body felt like mercury, heavy but fluid. It was very relaxing and enjoyable. I could relax the small pockets of non-fluids, which felt sharp and painful; then the fluid spread quickly until the sharpness was gone.

Experiences from childhood came back. I remembered walking home from grade school, looking down at the cracks in the sidewalk. The cracks flowed in perfect rhythm. Words, that at the time, I thought were to a stupid country song, began repeating in rhythm with the cracks. I was going into a trance. This frightened me, so I looked straight ahead, which brought me back to normal.

I also remembered, from childhood, sending blessings out to everyone in the world, and dreaming I was falling into a bottomless pit.

In August of 1971, I got the chance to go to a TM retreat in Arcata in Northern California, on the campus of Humboldt State College. The founder of TM, Maharishi Mahesh Yogi, would be there. Maharishi had been a teacher of celebrities—including the Beatles, Mia Farrow, and Donovan, but I didn't know this until several years later.

I hitchhiked into Arcata. The little town was nestled between the ocean and the Redwood Mountains. There were two health food stores, and every man seemed to have a beard and a dog.

I was there a little early. Walking through town, a nice girl in a Volkswagen asked me if I needed a ride. I told her of my situation. She said I could stay with her until the retreat started.

She worked for a professor and lived in a small house in back of his. There was an organic garden. The natural fragrances were enhanced by the crisp mountain air. She had two ducks. They would come to her when called, stand on her feet, and bend their necks back. She would then gently stroke their necks.

The retreat started August 8th. I learned the physical sequence (Hatha Yoga) that went with the meditation. There were lectures, times for meditation and Hatha, and wonderful meals.

Early one morning I woke up suddenly. I'm strong and very aware. I open my eyes. There are screens of wonderful vivid colors, suspended in the air. There are about twelve of them, one behind the other. I look at just one, and that one comes into focus, as the others become transparent. Each has a unique design of brilliant colors, changing form continuously in fluid artistic motions. I'm mesmerized by the screens for several minutes, and then faintly hear this exquisite music, as all the screens fade away completely.

The music is coming from the courtyard outside my window. My first reaction is, "I must be in heaven."

Quickly I dress, hurry into the courtyard, and sit quietly among the musicians. There are five or six musicians, guitars, a dulcimer, and a flute or two. One song is the Beatles song, *Black Bird*.

All the music has depth, creativity, and is flawlessly played. I feel like I'm sitting with the court musicians, a century or more in the past. We slowly swell to about fifteen people. The music lasts about two hours.

I heard later that some of the musicians were asked to leave, because they were getting attention that distracted from the purpose of the retreat—that they were from the music group, *The Beach Boys*.

This is all incredibly relaxing, and I feel very strong. Walking past the football field, I feel the impulse to run, like a child feels, just the energy bubbling out. I run about twenty yards, and stop exhausted. My heart is pounding. I have trouble getting my breath. Being a sports junkie, always physically active, I've never experienced anything like this. It's frightening, but my impulse is to just calm down. I relax, walk on, and forget the experience.

I overheard some people saying the staff was hiring workers for a longer meditation course. The course was to be in Majorca. I was too embarrassed to ask where Majorca is. This seemed like a rare opportunity. I immediately searched and found the hiring location. After a brief interview, they hired me as a cook, as I had some experience cooking, and knew something of healthy food. I didn't find out 'till later that Majorca's the largest of Spain's Balearic Islands in the Mediterranean. Being a poor man, my relatives back in Indiana at first didn't believe me, when I told them that I was going to live in the Mediterranean.

While writing this book thirty-seven years later, I ran into a full, large notebook that I had written that August in 1971. The first few pages were incoherent, but I read on. Then some jewels emerged, though I am not sure who said what; and sometimes, Maharishi would speak in pigeon English. Bearing all this in mind, here are some of my old notes. The course started **August 8, 1971**. On **August 9th** I gave Maharishi a rose and said, "*Jai Guru Dev*", as was the custom. His eyes twinkled slightly and he said, "*Jai Guru Dev*" back. **August 10th in the morning**, Maharishi said if course held in a cheap place, hippies would come and no good people.

August 10th in the evening: It is our responsibility for the well being for thousands of generations. ♦ Don't enjoy the fruit so much that you don't water the root. ♦ Nothing is an accident. An accident only indicates ignorance of the cause. ♦ The free will of man is a feature that goes on automatic. In man's infinite freedom, man can do anything. ♦ All is in the design of the creator. The simplicity of design is that all complexities come up naturally. ♦ Laws are set, but we can change the environment and thus change the laws. ♦ The force of nature (evolution) will not allow drug use for very long. Cause of use of drugs is lack of knowledge of life. ♦ Nothing is so important as gaining Cosmic Consciousness. From Cosmic Consciousness is the real joy of living. From Cosmic Consciousness comes God Consciousness, then Unity ♦ Go by the heart more than the doctor. ♦ At basis of problem is the weakness of man. Solution to all problems of life is strengthening life. ♦ Don't waste time in criticizing.

Wednesday morning, August 11: Every aspect of the tree is helped by attending to the root.

Wednesday night, August 11: It's a waste of time to think of single problems—impossible to decide on an intellectual level. ♦ Second and third techniques are fertilizer—makes growth faster and further. ♦ TM is transcending the mantra. ♦ Cause of rebirth is deep rooted stress. ♦ In Cosmic Consciousness, how or why would the body die? ♦ Faith with substantial basis is devotion. ♦ Right action does not cause stress. ♦ Suffering or wrong is not part of life, it has been superimposed. ♦ No one can go in the opposite direction of evolution for very long. ♦ Meditation is soothing to animals—produces warmer air. Animals feel and want to stay in the house. ♦ Maharishi knows where everyone is seated.

Thursday morning, August 12: The hymns of the Vedas are not written by human beings, but by the Creator or Creation. ♦ Main difference between objective and subjective—it is not possible to have full understanding from objective observation. ♦ The purpose of history is to inspire toward evolution and gain reality of life. Memorizing who and when is not important. Knowledge is not useful if bulk to gain is so great that it takes so long to gain and cannot live the knowledge.

Thursday night, August 12: In the transcendent are structured the hymns of the Vedas. ♦ Only answer questions when asked, thus know asker is ready. ♦ Maharishi is he who applies those truths to life. ♦ Endless is the Vedas. ♦ TM is practical way to live the wisdom of the Vedas. ♦ Let the mind be what it is. ♦ The Vedas will continue through different creations. ♦ Knowledge is never gained through reading, but through being. ♦ Destiny only moves the unstable. The stable move themselves. ♦ Infinity is everywhere, so starting from anywhere can get you there.

Friday morning, August 13: When the military has full use of creative intelligence, peace will be a reality. When weakness is gone, peace prevails. ♦ The experience of the transcendent is always subjective. ♦ Both intellectual and experience are necessary. Doesn't matter what one wants first—will seek the other later. ♦ The confusion when first coming into Cosmic Consciousness, because of reaching infinity, having no boundaries. ♦ When in activity don't try to remain in Being—would be dividing the mind, and the mind looses strength—this is mood making and it doesn't maintain the state of self but the *thought* of self. ♦ Plunge fully in both directions—TM and activity. ♦ Repeating thought of God arouses emotion of God only—this is pure hypnosis. The purpose of thought ends when it arouses us to experience the thought. ♦ The reality is with us always. ♦ Exposure to boundaries of activity fades Being. ♦ Meditation is natural. ♦ If I had known the West had bad connotations on meditation, would have called it something else—added transcendental to clarify. ♦ Science of Creative Intelligence (SCI) sounds more modern. ♦ It is the benefit not the name or understanding that has spread. ♦ Loosing is the path of gaining—this is the path of love—loose all and are full with the technique of TM. ♦ If in higher states once, one will know the path of TM and will start to spread it.

Friday night, August 13: There is disagreement among seekers of truth because they have not found it. ♦ Music is life, is a wave of life, if is good one forgets everything. In TM one forgets everything. TM is the music of the soul. ♦ We should depend on our own decisions. No other knows the whole story about one's self. ♦ Only the truth continues. ♦ A meditator can find the reality of the Bible—the words are there—the meaning belongs to the level of consciousness. ♦ Teachers learn more, thus speed transcending. ♦ Mantra on level of transcending thought is very powerful. It's beyond us to understand fully—also not enough time. ♦ Brain is someplace, mind is everywhere. ♦ With TM the hardness of the heart softens and love begins. Unbounded waves of love are called devotion. Slight breeze when heart softened will cause tidal wave of love. ♦ Nothing is allowed not to fit in the divine plan—the rose has a thorn. ♦ Cosmic Consciousness or pure conscious is the only state in which love can be unbounded.

Saturday morning, August 14: Study in depth in one field brings awareness of everything and makes one feel at home everywhere. ♦ To spread TM to church, talk of TM not religion. Say church saves one from doing gross wrong. Don't mention religion in introductory lecture. ♦ If we have negative feelings toward someone we can make them negative. ♦ Men change, so if you remember what they said and it was negative you are doing that man harm. ♦ There could be a non-meditator who could be evolved to 90% potential, or someone meditating long may have 20%. Meditator goes faster but may have been born on a different level. ♦ It's not possible to judge others advancement. ♦ World was created because fullness wanted to flow.

Saturday night, August 14: When the body is polluted, our perception is lost, and we lose awareness of our essential nature. ♦ One in knowledge cannot understand one in ignorance. ♦ The origin of sin is going to the relative to understand sin, knowing that the ultimate will bring one back. The closer one gets back one regains the feeling that one has never left. ♦ Different states of consciousness are different degrees of the unmanifest, or the scheme of nature, the need to be multiple. Some call it the *Play of the Divine*. ♦ The relative's grip on us makes us fear letting go of our boundaries, which stops us from getting back to infinity. ♦ Ignorance of the relative also causes sin. ♦ The tree is in the seed. Nothing has ever been lost. ♦ Ignorance doesn't exist—it has no reality. The sense of loss is a non-reality, yet it is experienced, like a mirage. The unbounded omnipresent cannot be covered by anything. Ignorance cannot be substantiated, because it doesn't exist. Knowledge can be located. ♦ What is real is continuance and fullness of life. Evolution has a purpose of fullness. ♦ When with people talk on their level or appear to be a fool and confuse others. ♦ In one state one doesn't feel suffering. ♦ Should not appear abnormal in any way, so message will spread. First impression is the last impression. When we remove the ignorance from society, then we will do what we want. ♦ Can meditate three times a day if have nothing else to do. If sick need meditation more.

Sunday morning, August 15: The present destruction is creating a new finer existence. ♦ Whispers are more powerful than shouts. ♦ The speed of light is the only constant.

Sunday night, August 15: If go fast in outer space, time goes slower; but people who stay on Earth will age faster. ♦ Mass decides what a star is—mass attracts planets and draws their energy. ♦ Light leaving a large mass would be drawn back and maybe not even leave— this is called a black hole. ♦ If have absolute can know anything at will. ♦ Time is different in different levels of consciousness. ♦ Should have understanding of the relative as much as possible. ♦ The letters of Sanskrit are pure Being. ♦ "Ah" is the seed of the seed. "Ga" is second degree of manifestation. "Nee" is third degree of manifestation. ♦ The Rig Veda is the textbook of the Science of Creative Intelligence (SCI).

♦ Bhagavad Gita is the practical technique to gain knowledge. ♦ The cognition of ignorance is knowledge.

Monday morning, August 16: It's very stressful to try to leave your body. ♦ You can't be totally objective because the self is involved. ♦ We are in a mingled state when objectivity overshadows subjectivity. ♦ My seed is always in infinity. ♦ You can't be where you are. You must be a step ahead—willingly or unwillingly. ♦ TM is the ladder. The instructor and organization may remain on the ground. ♦ There is a movement from Indonesia called Subud, lead by a man who supposedly has direct contact with God. I think it is a spirit taking over man's nervous system—thus slows evolution. ♦ Lesser desires are found in dullness of life. ♦ A group from Chicago says they have the original TM. ♦ You could transcend by going into subtler levels of smell or taste. The value of transcending by mantra has added value of life supporting influences. Others methods are slower. ♦ If it is useful, you remember it. ♦ Keeping a 5 pm appointment in our mind for a long time is a waste of energy—in Cosmic Consciousness deal with one thing at a time and the right time. ♦ Once in the home, enjoy the home, and forget how we got there. ♦ Don't fix mind on anything, just take in what's passing, otherwise, more exertion than results. ♦ Concentrated energy could cause harm if body not ready. ♦ Even in going to the South one will eventually reach the North. ♦ Accept all that Kundalini Yoga says. ♦ Yoga is the philosophy of union of mind and body, which extends to maximum use of environment. ♦ One could start from anywhere and achieve the goal, so have many systems of Yoga. If one is perfect in culture of any one aspect of life, this would enhance the others— this is Yoga. ♦ You could start with the body, prana (breath), or the environment. ♦ Life is never in isolation, all is integrated. ♦ Hatha (the physical Yoga) means force. ♦ You can combine two systems or three etc., or all. ♦ Patanjali's Yoga has eight limbs (the eight aspects of life to integrate)—has been misinterpreted to mean eight steps. ♦ Behavioral aspects of Yoga cannot be practiced, only achieved naturally when in Cosmic Consciousness. ♦ Harmony dominates and differences are insignificant in Unity Consciousness. ♦ In all states of consciousness the self awareness is the same. ♦ Knowledge and experience are closely related.

Tuesday morning, August 17: Unity is restful dynamism. On that level is hardly any difference between action and achievement. ♦ In Unity the infinity of the object is perceived. In Cosmic Consciousness the infinity of the self is perceived. ♦ In Unity the boundary of the self is porous or can enjoy full value of infinity. ♦ Time will come when just can't behave negatively—this creation is expression of bliss. ♦ In the first moment of the flash of "*I Am That*" it is overwhelming, then one becomes more established in Unity. One realizes that he is this and that, both. ♦ In TM one transcends boundaries. The other side, the transcendental, is really what we are. ♦ Let differences live spontaneously on the level of harmony.

Tuesday night, August 17: One creates in oneself the perception, and then the master says, "That is it." ♦ God Consciousness is the finest relative—greater than Cosmic Consciousness, but less than Unity. ♦ Supreme knowledge is beyond the relative, thus no words. Brahma Sutras are then a great help. ♦ Between teacher and his masters is the greatest bond of love that could ever be. ♦ Body—I am devotee, mind—I am a part of thee. ♦ In God consciousness there is no difference between devotee and God. In Unity the difference is lost. ♦ God embraces the devotee—at that state, the devotee has no desire to unite with God because serving is so fulfilling. ♦ It's the Grace of God that Unity descends on the devotee. ♦ Glory to the master who has shown me my God.

Wednesday morning, August 18: *Yama* is the administration. *Niyama* is the law that leads the administration. *Asana* is the stable aspect of Yoga union. *Dyana* is meditation or spontaneous refinement. *Being* is the stationary ego or non-functioning. *Samadhi* is even, steady intelligence.

Thursday night, August 19: To Christians—one man can belong to many clubs, but doesn't attend them all at the same time. ♦ Feel freshness after silence. ♦ Amness is individual with boundaries. Isness is life. ♦ Jesus freaks is self deception. I am maintaining my mood, staying in the relative, keeping individuality, and thinking of surrender—make a man dull. ♦ Christ will come when less stress in the world. ♦ If a man commits suicide he remains bewildered in the air for a very long time, doesn't advance. Worst thing a man can do for himself or anyone else. ♦

Living alone is only possible in the state of fulfillment. ♦ *Tapas* is heat, radiation, and the glow of life; from going inward (not from austerity). ♦ Non-possessing maintains the continuity of *Being*. ♦ The whole of relativity belongs to the three *Gunas*—dullness, activity, refinement. ♦ When to steal is on the basis of two—it doesn't promote Unity. ♦ *Brahmacharya* is living eternal freedom. ♦ Experience what you like; don't experience what you don't like. ♦ *Svad* is closing the chapter of the world, and opening one's awareness to the self. ♦ *Asana* pose is establishing the individuality in the never changing. ♦ Need all eight limbs of Yoga to maintain life in its full value. ♦ Anything that should be done tomorrow, should be done today.

Friday morning, August 20: Education is expansion of consciousness. ♦ Teach the esoteric to the child—gives him criteria for life—the basis is the mantra. ♦ To use a word requires all parts of the brain, most involved thing a man can do. ♦ TM studies show radical positive changes in life plus increase in alpha waves and ability to turn them off.

Friday night, August 20: Devotion is the impulse of a melting heart rising up in waves of love. When ice is melted even a slight breeze produces a wave. ♦ When one can appreciate every item of creation deeply, then one can appreciate the artist … God. Devotion isn't practiced. It is the spontaneous ability to appreciate even the minutest detail. ♦ I will sometime talk of Siva Sutras, Brahma Sutras, remainder of Bhagavad Gita, and the Vedas—beautiful knowledge in all these areas. ♦ The answer lies in sensitivity. Sensitivity lies in TM. ♦ If one is calm and quiet, one will have a wider lens, and can comprehend more items—thus have better results. ♦ If you sit fulfilled, the awareness is unbounded. ♦ Lesser activity is more pleasureful to the mind. ♦ Dig a foundation—silence for activity. ♦ In TM the mind is non-active, but alert. This is preparing the actor for action. Do less and accomplish more. ♦ All the problems of life belong to the weakness of the mind. If the knower doesn't know himself, the knowledge is baseless—it's a mirage.

Saturday night, August 21: TM is the most easily taught and the most publicly available means to change our consciousness. ♦ Our awareness is below what it could be. ♦ We are easily hypnotized from birth through our education. TM can neutralize this. ♦ We have made subconscious errors of perception in our early years, but now we think we make super conscious decisions. ♦ The closest we can come to understanding is in our own selves. ♦ Lesser beliefs, like in the Sufi traditions, may be locked up or may just play the game in an extraordinary way. ♦ Impersonal love is over-flow of personal love. ♦ Rapid change hurts until we must move. ♦ Getting away from the garden is the same as going to the house—our choice is which way to look at it—pain or joy. ♦ We should work for evolution and not mind the destruction. Nature has taught that destruction and creation go on simultaneously. To bother about the destruction causes more destruction. ♦ We don't forget in Cosmic Consciousness. We just don't waste energy on unnecessary or repeating thoughts. ♦ In the new paradigm, the differences are part of life, but because we breath fuller, the differences will fade away and harmony will dominate.

Saturday at 3:50 pm, August 21: Some meditators were reading *The Hobbit* and *The Lord of the Rings* by Tolkien. ♦ Creative individuals can relate themselves to the cosmos. ♦ The wilderness mimics freedom. ♦ The finer has waves, but the grosser seems to have particles. ♦ Light is a vacuum—has nothing in it. ♦ Brain waves acting together in TM make it possible for super-conductivity. ♦ Vacuum is pure Being. ♦ Energy levels are more spaced at subtle levels. ♦ Well begun is half done. ♦ Language of any part could describe Being, because Being is the basis of everything.

Saturday night, August 21: TM is restful alertness, unbounded awareness—the basic field of creative intelligence. ♦ TM comes naturally because the nature of the mind is to cast off stress, and the nature of the body is to throw off foreign materials. ♦ The nature of the mind is to expand and enjoy. ♦ If you have high blood pressure, creative intelligence is low. ♦ If a man is unhealthy, certainly he has become less intelligent. ♦ Intelligence and creative intelligence are directly related. ♦ There is no mental disease other than a bad self image. ♦ If Maharishi forgets something, it was bad. ♦ The greatest creative phenomenon are TM and landing on the moon.

Sunday morning, August 22: The star of Bethlehem was an exploding star.

Monday morning, August 23: With TM fewer resources are necessary for happiness. ♦ Brain was once for solving problems, but now is for enjoying life.

Monday evening, August 23: When conditioned thought is rethought and no punishment is given, then conditioning is broke. ♦ We can't handle some thoughts directly. ♦ The waves of Karma are unfathomable. ♦ Be one-pointed in Majorca. ♦ Don't base life on momentary impulses. ♦ We take life so lightly (superficially) that we miss it's depth. ♦ I don't think that headbands are appropriate. I don't like ties, but we have a responsibility to the organization. I would rather disband my movement than have teachers of your appearance. ♦ Don't socialize with other meditators while in Majorca.

The course ended and the long bus ride back to Indiana began. I was reading a book that many others at the course were reading: *Autobiography of a Yogi* by Paramahansa Yogananda.

I ran out of money and was hungry.

We had a brief stop. I walked across the street into a supermarket. I was beginning to rationalize stealing some food, but quickly to my mind, came what I had just read. I had read that God supplies all needs—so I didn't steal.

Back on the bus, I met two young men who were interested in meditation. I told them what little I knew. They gave me some money as they got off the bus. I hadn't asked for it; and it was given with such a consciousness, that to turn it down would have been an insult. I ate at the next stop.

Traveling by plane, I left New York for Majorca on October 17, 1971. I was to work as a cook, for room and board for six months; then for three months, I'd take the Teacher Training Course.

I met other meditators on the plane, interesting people from all over the United States.

There were buses waiting for us at the airport in Majorca. We drove along small winding roads, by lemon trees and ancient stone walls. Everything looked and smelled too perfect to be real. It was already more than I expected. The air was pure, crisp, and alive.

I was told we'd work a normal forty hour week. We actually were working eleven hours a day, seven days a week. It was so great a blessing to be there that I never heard anyone complain.

While pealing fruit, the knife slipped and I was almost cut! This jolted me awake. I looked around. Everyone was drowsy looking. This could be dangerous. I mentioned this to my supervisor—she wasn't even interested. I told her I was taking the next weekend off. Others followed suit. More people were hired and our hours were cut. She acted as if I had done something wrong.

I worked various kitchen jobs and did carpentry, but my best job was working with the children—about twenty-two kids from five to eight, with one, twelve-year old who came and went on his own.

The little darlings forced me to live in the present. They were from various countries and lifestyles, so this was a big adjustment for them. I tried to be gentle, yet protecting, and consistent.

One little, red-headed girl, Zoe, had a particularly difficult time adjusting. She would cry loud and often. The other workers, four ladies, couldn't get her to stop. When she was calm, I'd take her from her crib. If she started to cry, I'd take her back. She eventually got so use to me, that when she cried one of the others would come and get me; I'd go to her crib, reach out to her, and she'd stop crying immediately.

It would sometimes get tense with all of us in one small room, so I'd diffuse the tension by taking some of the children to a small playground or for a walk. On one walk, one of the boys said he'd like to go to the candy bar trees. I thought he was joking, but went that direction anyway, just for a change of pace. There I found my first carob trees. Carob's inside a pod about the size of a green bean, and tastes like chocolate. John the Baptist ate it. The Bible calls it wild locust.

On one walk, the older boy joined us. He was very muscular and athletic for his age. He climbed the dangerous rocks and swam into the underground caves. He was a hero to the little ones.

On that walk, we were twenty yards from the sea—much closer than usual. The older boy went to climb on the rocks. Some of the children followed him. I told him to come back. He kept going. I told the children to come back. They too kept going. This was the first time they disobeyed me. I was scared! The children could easily die from falling off the rocks into the crushing waves below. I used a firmer tone to the children. They kept going. Now they were so far from me that I couldn't physically stop them all. I ran and grabbed the older boy and spanked him hard—or rather, what seemed hard to the little ones. The children finally listened to me. I never took them that close again, no matter how much they pleaded.

One of the hotel staff had a little girl who would sometimes come and play with us. My supervisor told me they were concerned about the insurance, so I had to tell this child she couldn't come into the playroom. After telling her, she got very upset, pointed her finger at me, and said that I was very bad.

Once I took the children to a little playground nearby. I was just sitting and watching. A ritual with Maharishi was to bring flowers to him. Several of the children were picking wild flowers and bringing them to me.

My job was changed to building furniture. Once when I was walking along the street, the children were walking on the other side. Zoe ran out of the group, across the street, hugged my leg, and then ran back.

A lot of the people were reading *The Hobbit*, by J.R.R. Tolkien, and then Tolkien's trilogy, *The Lord of the Rings*. I was in such a hypersensitive condition from the meditating, that I couldn't sleep after reading a negative section. I would have to read through until I reached a positive section—even if it took all night.

I became close friends with two Scandinavians. John was from Finland. He played guitar, sang, walked on his hands, and spoke nine languages. Hans was Swedish. He could also walk on his hands, and spoke ten languages. Hans was so strong and calm, that even the women who hated men would fall in love with him.

We became characters from Tolkien's books. I was Gandalf, the human wizard; because I could juggle, knew Kundalini Yoga, and got to choose first. John became Frodo, the young Hobbit. Hans was Bilbo, the older Hobbit. We would go on adventures. If one of us had enough nerve to do something, the others would follow. It was all good-natured fun, yet sometimes it became dangerous. We would sometimes take ropes, blankets, and candles, which we never used.

Our most common adventure was exploring caves. Looking out

from the island's coast onto the sea, there was often a twenty yard drop to the water below, though sometimes less, and even an occasional beach. We would climb down the cliffs; sometimes find hidden caves, although some of the caves were not hidden.

The first cave we discovered started as an easy climb; then squeezed into a two foot square, open on the left, with a sheer drop some twenty yards to the water below. The square continued for two yards, then ended with another sheer drop. We had to turn slowly in the square so the feet came out first. To the right was a crevice just the right height and size to grip with the hands. Walking with the hands for about two yards, we could easily drop to a platform leading into several room-like caves.

A lot of people wanted to go with us. Most stopped once they saw the square. Only one girl went in. She hated men—except Hans, of course.

Another cave was at the tip of an inward pointing "V". The only way to enter was from an outer edge. We had to crawl some thirty yards, with the water only a few inches away. Inside was a small pool of water with a stalactite hanging directly above it. The stalactite rhythmically dripped into the pool, pushing deep clear ripples across the otherwise calm water. As the sun rose, its rays reflected off of the ripples—forming clear bright rainbows, about four inches thick, covering the whole surface of the cave.

Another cave had a land opening that appeared to be drilled, because it was so symmetrical. It was circular with a diameter of about three feet, going down some thirty yards at a 45° angle. Crawling into the darkness feet first was very slow and awkward. As my eyes adjusted, far off to the lower right a dim light was growing brighter, illuminating a huge cavern at least the size of two football fields. My ledge was about three feet square and some forty yards above the water. My relative smallness crept in, with accompanying fear and fresh ideas of adventure. Could I get out? How stable is this ledge? This would be a good place to hide treasure. I crawled out. It wasn't too difficult.

We often got back past the evening meal. The night watchman didn't understand that we had a right to feed ourselves. Our organization had purchased all the food. We'd climb onto the highest roof and drop into the kitchen from a small window that wouldn't lock. We'd usually fix cheese sandwiches. The other hotel staff made fun of the watchman, because he couldn't read or write; but he was very perceptive, and one of only two adults I ever saw Maharishi give flowers to. Maharishi gave flowers to all the children.

There were incredible daily lectures by Maharishi. After a particularly inspiring one, when I left feeling a oneness with all humanity, I decided to talk to some of the other Americans whom I'd met on the plane flying in. Their interpretation shocked me. They believed the main point of the lecture was that Maharishi's meditation technique was the only valid path, and thus all others were of no value. Their conclusion was almost the opposite of mine. John called these people *bliss-ninnies.* He once introduced me saying I was an American but didn't act like one—meaning I wasn't a bliss-ninnie.

Three of the other meditators were actually from my hometown. Which is even more surprising, when you consider that when I left Evansville I didn't even know anyone else there that meditated? They are Michael and Teresa Banser and Teresa's brother Charley Mattingly. Years later, I ran into Michael and Teresa in Evansville and once even saw Charlie in Lawrence, Kansas.

One of the people who hung out with us was a very pretty, gentle, and stable lady, who I'd met when I was a server in the food line. I had guessed her to be in her mid-twenties. Her manners and gracefulness, and the artistic way she dressed were impressive. She was the granddaughter of the Olsons. They were the family that Maharishi stayed with in the United States when he first arrived.

There was a side room in one of the hotels where the owners allowed the locals to hold church services. I tried to meditate in this room, but found it strangely difficult. I took the Olson's granddaughter there to see how she'd react. She walked in just a few steps, said she couldn't meditate there, and we left. She was more aware than I was.

One afternoon people were running around in a frenzy. The Olsons were worried because their granddaughter was past her curfew. It was then that I found out she was only thirteen. She came back safely, and had just lost track of time.

Once, Hans and I climbed one of the mountains. It was a one-day trip, if you left early, walked fast, and got back late. At the beginning there was a path. Later on just faded marks on rocks. As you walked you got progressively more tired and hot; but, at the same time, the air got cooler and invigorating, so the conditions for climbing were perfect.

At one point, we were walking a thin path with very small trees to the sides. In front of us appeared two very large wild boars. They looked straight at us, with no fear. We very quickly, but softly, walked off the path. The boars continued their walk past us. Hans remarked, "That was a real adventure!"

At the top of the mountain there was a little snow on the ground. We could see the whole island. A few clouds were below us, as if they were attached to the mountain. About a hundred yards around us and twenty yards below, an eagle soared.

There was a carnival of activities outside the official meditations and discourses—beaches, mountains, beautiful girls, guitar playing (by John), bonfires, simple walks, and dancing.

As a child, I had become extremely ill for several days. I became so hypersensitive a whisper was an unbearable yell. The light of an ordinary light bulb seemed blinding like the sun. I walked with fear and uncertainty, even slower than my grandmother.

This illness recurred in Majorca, only worse. This time, I was so engulfed with pain, that walking slowly, the pressure of my feet touching the floor caused pain all the way to the top of my head. I lost all mental bearing. I lost track of time. I often didn't know where I was, though I stayed only in my apartment. I got lost on the way to the bathroom, and even forgot where I was trying to go. I tried to leave the apartment, but couldn't find the door.

Finally I made it out. People are waiting for Maharishi to arrive for a lecture, about a hundred yards from my room. Half way there is a tiny flower shop. I feel like a zombie staggering into the shop. From the door my vision is drawn to a single purple rose. It's bright, deep, and magical, the only color in a black and white scene. Somehow, I buy the rose.

I walk to the entrance of the lecture hall, where there are two lines of people waiting with flowers in hand for Maharishi to walk between them. One line is slightly shorter. I walk and stand at the end of that line. Just then Maharishi's limousine pulls up. Maharishi gets out, but instead of going to the closer, longer line, comes straight to me. I turn facing him, with the purple rose held lightly between my hands. Usually Maharishi walks briskly, taking flowers, and quickly repeats, "*Jai Guru Dev.*" This time, he looks me straight in the eye and very slowly says, "*Jai … Guru … Dev.*" The next thing I remember, I'm turned facing the lecture hall, the flower's gone, and I am strong and clear.

I feel a vacuum behind Maharishi gently pull me in. I'm guided to the last row, to the only empty seat inside the large, crowded lecture hall. I close my eyes, relax, and don't try to listen. When Maharishi's words seem to be meant for me, I hear them clearly, as if he's several feet in front of me.

Maharishi would give me messages with his eyes. Once I had a crush on a pretty, but shallow, French girl. I stood with her in line as Maharishi passed. He looked at me, then her, then gave me a stern disapproving glance. He was always right. This made it scary if I was misbehaving, but wonderful if I sincerely wanted to grow.

Once Maharishi looked at me, then down some twenty people to a lady I didn't know, and then back to me. I looked for her inside the lecture hall, but couldn't find her.

After the lecture I looked again, briefly. For some reason, I walked upstairs to an overcrowded lounge. People were standing shoulder-to-shoulder with very few seats and no empty ones. I began to feel a pressure at the third eye point (above the nose a couple of inches and inside slightly) as I moved. As I stopped from the pressure, I pivoted and found a direction where there was no pressure. I would then walk in the pressure-less direction. In this way, I was guided through the crowd to an empty seat. Seated several feet directly in front of me, was the lady. I was stunned, but shortly caught myself, and began to casually speak to her. At first she seemed ordinary and I couldn't figure any purpose for this meeting. Slowly an interesting and unique personality emerged, yet we were very different and I still couldn't find a purpose for this encounter.

When I was about eighteen, on one of my first dates, I had this very strange experience. At that time, an awkward silence came to our conversation. I asked for her hands, held them loosely, closed my eyes, and relaxed. A mental image of vibrations came to me. I analyzed them and seemed to come up with knowledge of her past and future. Every few years this would happen again.

It happened spontaneously with this lady on Majorca. She first thought it was a joke. I told her things about her parents that no one else knew. She got mad and left. I then realized that this little gift didn't really do any good, or so it seemed at the time. I've rarely done it since, and never as accurate as that time.

To get a private audience with Maharishi there was a chain of command, but it was almost impossible to see him that way. One could simply speak as Maharishi walked by; but most people couldn't do this because of fear, shyness, or they would simply space out in his presence. There was a blissful timelessness when you were next to him ... problems would dissolve.

I had a reputation, though only partially deserved, of being able to speak directly to Maharishi. Once, I accumulated several people's questions; so I went to see him, happy to have an excuse to be in his presence. I was pushed by others needs, though fearful I'd disappoint them.

I took an elevator to Maharishi's floor. Some fifty people are in the small lobby. Maharishi is trying to leave on the other elevator, as everyone there wants some of his time. One lady emerges from the crowd. Maharishi says to her, "I don't have time for the questions, but the answers are yes and yes." Maharishi then looks directly at me, saying, "I'll be back in one hour."

I wait for about two hours, then go quickly down to the kitchen to grab a snack. I hurry back, anxiously riding the elevator, and step quickly out into the lobby. Mararishi is standing at the entrance to the small hallway leading to his room; again, there are some fifty people between us. I walk forward, anyway ... an opening appears in the crowd. I float effortlessly through the opening, then stand facing Maharishi. Out of me comes one sentence. Maharishi tells me to take the problems to one of his assistants. I do so, and all the problems are solved.

Each sunset was spectacular as the sun dipped behind the clouds ringing the mountain tops. Once, I was watching this show while washing fruit in the large kitchen sinks. There appears to my left a magenta (reddish purple) statue. It's some four feet of the floor, about four feet wide, and five feet tall. It consists of an ornate throne with someone sitting motionless, cross-legged on the throne, all in magenta. I turn my head towards the statue. It disappears. I'm thinking that I must have imagined it. I return to my work. The statue reappears. This time, I turn my head slower. The statue dissolves with my turning. I return to my work, thinking that I've imagined it again. It comes a third time. This time I keep my head straight and slowly look to the left. The statue stays. There are no movements or insights. I experience some eyestrain, so return to my work. When I look back, the statue's gone.

There were a couple of days in which I was overcome by intense physical pain and obsessive negative thoughts. I felt suffocated in my room. I was compelled to walk to a close, small beach. I'm walking slowly along a dirt road to that beach. The pain isn't lessening. I'm trying to relax and find an answer. I remember having read recently that the best way to neutralize negative thoughts is simply to bring in positive ones. This book further suggested imagining yourself sitting in the heart of the person you feel the most positive about. I imagine myself sitting in the heart of Jesus, radiating love in all directions. Instantly, my pain and negativity are gone. Love, lightness, and strength are all there is.

In the spring of 1972 we left Majorca for Fiuggi, Italy, fifty kilometers (thirty-one miles) south of Rome, in the mountains.

I was then free of work obligations, so could just do as I pleased. We meditated, made music, went for walks, listened to Maharishi's lectures, talked, climbed the mountains, juggled, walked on our hands, rode the train into Rome, and just simply enjoyed. Even playing chess or pinball machines carried on a mystical air. Of course, romances flourished.

John's friend, Annu, came from Finland. She was stunningly beautiful, but had such a sensitivity and depth that I'd sometimes forget her external beauty.

Once I sat in my room to meditate, but the thought of Annu coming into my room was so strong I couldn't focus. I turned to look at the door, expecting to see her. I felt foolish, as there had been no knock or noise. I would have heard the door opening. Again, I tried to meditate. The door opened and Annu walked in. She had been living several blocks away, but unbeknownst to me had just moved into the hotel next door. She had been trying to meditate, but the thought of coming into my room was so strong that she couldn't focus.

Once I ran into Annu, accidently, on the street. My shoulder was hurting. Somehow, I knew she could heal me. I asked her to relax and search her body for pain. She said she had no pain, but closed her eyes and searched anyway. She found pain in her shoulder. I asked her to relax her pain as I relaxed mine. Both pains disappeared.

Once Annu, myself, and two others were sitting at a sidewalk café. Maharishi had said that one thing we should never do when meditating is to drink wine. I had read that Malaga wine is the healthiest alcohol in the world. The café had Malaga. It was too tempting not to try, just once. I took a small sip, swallowed, and was immediately out of my body. About three feet in the air, looking down, I saw Annu controlling me like I was a puppet, but it didn't seem to matter—being with a woman as beautiful as Annu is worth losing some freedom. Then just as quickly, I was back into the body.

There was one man the others didn't like much. He was the only one to drink regularly, and the first to drop out of teacher training. His clothes were sloppy looking and didn't match. He would sit by himself and stare—but, I felt a pleasant strength when I was close to him. I went out of my way to know him. We became friends.

Once, while we were walking down a gravel road, he confided in me, saying he could go into other dimensions that were as real as this one. I had never heard or thought of anything like this. I relaxed deeper, to absorb what he was saying. I absentmindedly picked up a handful of small jagged rocks. There were fence posts about five feet high and ten feet apart, running parallel with the road, about twenty feet away. The top was about (2x2½) inches. I threw a rock at the nearest fence post, which had a bush beside it. The rock hit directly on top of that fence post. We continued walking. I threw another rock, hitting the same spot on the same fence post. This happened two more times. Then on the fifth throw, I was so far away that I had to wind up like a baseball pitcher to generate enough force to reach the fence post ... again, I hit the same spot! Startled, I stopped. This seemed impossible. The intellect came in. I was going to analyze what had happened. I threw some thirty rocks, but couldn't come within six feet of my target. Reflecting on this later, it seemed that I was so deep and pure that what I willed came true; at least partly, because I was not attached to the result.

Once, some of us went to visit Naples and Mt. Vesuvius. We drove up the volcano as far as the car could go. We were tired and it was late, so slept in the car. I woke before the others, walked to the top of the volcano, and looked in. It seemed to go down forever. There were small pockets of rising steam, with strong looking, easy climbing rocks, near the top. There was a sign beside me, in Italian. I started climbing down. I climbed for about an hour in a zigzagging fashion and then reached a bad angle with my head farther out than my feet. My handholds began to crumble! I thrust the body into the rocks! There were no thoughts. To move a hand or foot, I'd distribute the weight evenly among the other three limbs. My head occasionally scraped the rocks—I'd ignore it. It took about an hour to go back up six feet to the solid rocks. All this time there were no thoughts. Once back at the car, I told my companions what happened. They didn't believe me.

The course ended at Fiuggi in June of 1972. I had assumed that the personal connection I had with Maharishi was shared with others, but talking to others, over the years, I have found this not to be the case. I hadn't qualified as a teacher.

Annu and I, traveled to Finland by train, ship, and hitchhiking. We traveled through Italy, Switzerland, Germany, Denmark, and Sweden. The train ride into Switzerland from the polluted plains of Northern Italy gave a rush of fresh air and energy as young students going home for the weekend darted in and out of each cabin looking for their friends. Walking later in Switzerland, we stopped to rest at a large, empty town square surrounded by towering, ancient buildings. A young man came up to me and asked if I would like to buy some shit. I assumed he didn't mean this literally, so asked to see it. He returned quickly with some hash (concentrated Marijuana). The square began to quickly fill with people setting up booths and a large stage. We were at the beginning of a once a year music festival. We walked around, finding smaller stages nearby, with more modern music. It got very crowded, so we left.

The boat ride from Sweden to Finland was very calm. I could see light around people's heads and shoulders. At that time, I couldn't see any colors in the light and had yet to hear of auras.

Once in Finland, the only job I could get, which even required pull, was as a busboy in a restaurant in downtown Helsinki. I worked a hard forty-hour week, dealing with obnoxious drunks and thick cigarette smoke for the equivalent of $125 dollars a month.

I got to spend some time in an abandoned house in Tampere. I could use the neighbor's sauna. My house was surrounded by berry bushes and edible mushrooms. I meditated often.

Once walking in the woods with Oke, he's a meditator whose family owned the sauna I used; I saw these surrealistic mushrooms, a yellow one six inches in diameter next to a much smaller yellow one. Several yards further were purple ones of the same sizes, then growing in the middle of the path a large white one with red polka dots. Oke told me the polka dotted ones were magic (poisonous) mushrooms that the gypsies say that if you look for one you can't find it, but if you run into one, that means you are ready for it. A little further on, I saw another magic mushroom growing inside a small bush. A tree about four feet tall grew from the center of the bush. This mushroom was perfectly protected.

Later we cleaned, dried, and smoked the mushrooms. Listening to the music of *Pink Floyd*, I could isolate each instrument. I became dizzy and sick at my stomach, opened the door, took several deep breaths, and felt good again.

Once in deep meditation, I re-experienced being five years old ... the feeling of complete faith, with no fear of being thrown high in the air. Even when dropped, the faith wasn't affected. I felt that if I didn't leave then, I'd never leave; so, the next morning I was gone.

I took a ship to Copenhagen, then went to the ticket office, walked up a long flight of stairs, opened the door, and walked in. I was stunned! On each side, sitting calmly was a small man with a machine gun! I looked straight ahead, walked at a normal pace, but past the offices and out the opposite door. Shortly, I found out it was because of the terrorism at the Olympics, which I didn't know of since I hadn't seen a newspaper in English in months.

My plane didn't leave for several days. I didn't have enough money for a hotel, so took my sleeping bag, looking for a place to crash. I found a park with nice big bushes; but, into the night, it got frighteningly cold. I went searching for a warmer place and found an unlocked restroom with a very hard floor, but no cold breezes, behind a large church. I slept intermittently and restlessly.

In the morning, I was awakened abruptly by a gruff voice from the door and blinding sunlight. Standing in the doorway was a muscular man in work clothes. The door shut swiftly, as I tried to tell him why I was there. I could then do nothing, but try to compose myself, and wait.

A policeman came, and off we went. He was efficient and pleasant, considering the circumstances. He got me on an earlier flight, escorting me past a long line of curious passengers, waiting in the boarding line. No one spoke to me during the flight.

I found, over the years (as have many others) that Maharishi's meditation technique is too much like a drug, so rarely use it. Though I have found that in times of extreme stress TM can be very effective for quick relaxation, and the basics do carry over to other meditations.

On October 28, 1972, my mother was initiated into TM at the University of Evansville. She told me her mantra, although she practiced it very little. She passed May 4, 1994. I had forgotten her mantra, yet at her funeral the mantra repeated clearly and rhythmically, for several minutes, in my head.

I finally reconnected with my friends from Europe in 2001. John and Annu married, and then divorced in 1975. Annu remarried, has five kids, and works in child care in downtown Helsinki. John remarried in 1976, and then divorced again in 1993. He has two grown daughters, Kaisa and Kirsi, and one grandson, Hiski, from that marriage. Since 1996 he's been with his girlfriend, Arja. John sold his software businesses, has a Masters Degree in Social Psychology, and has worked as a trainer in psychotherapies and Psychological Coaching.

Hans now lives in Japan with his wife Hiroko, who's a pharmacist, his son Anders, daughter Naomi, and dog Kuru. Hans teaches English. We write very often and I'm always excited to get one of his letters.

John and Hans are still intelligent, responsible, and spiritual, but still keep the lightness of those days ... even, on occasion, using the names Frodo and Bilbo, as I sometimes go by Gandalf.

Maharishi died February 5, 2008. I wrote Hans and reviewed all of my notes and records from when I was with Maharishi—expecting and hoping some message or blessing would come. Then I found the forgotten notebook from the course with Maharishi in Northern California in August, 1971.

I can never lose respect for Maharishi. His healing and guidance are permanently engraved in my mind.

Chapter Seven: Swami Rudrananda, the American Yogi

I lived for several months in Swami Rudrananda's Kundalini Yoga Ashram in Bloomington, Indiana, the college town of Indiana University. Rudi studied under Swami Nityananda, the great Indian saint, and others. Rudi was a large, powerful man, with sensitivity and caring to match.

I worked in the Ashram Construction Company. For one period, I was continuously tired. For another period, three hours sleep a night was all I needed.

The meditation was done upstairs. Then, sometimes, Rudi would sit downstairs with the rest of us scattered casually at his feet. On one such occasion, I was sitting, just watching, as many spoke softly among themselves. Rudi flicked has wrist towards the far corner. Some fifteen people in that area jerked in unison. Most of them were not looking at Rudi.

Rudi taught one main technique. I've since learned slight variations from other traditions. Its validity, simplicity, and power, are increasingly ingrained in me. Rudi believes that to intellectually understand is just the beginning—real growth must actually be achieved through sustained hard work. We must consciously surrender, deeper than outer circumstances, and keep the surrender active through movement through the chakras (the subtle wheels of pure energy that are the source of our physical being). For simplicity's sake, I'll just refer to this as Rudi's Technique.

When Rudi was gone Michael Shoemaker, later to become Swami Chetanananda, was in charge. Michael and I, and three others, were basketball players. Sometimes, after the evening meditation, we'd go to the university gym to play. We were an egoless precision unit, greater than the sum of our individual skills, a meditation in action.

There were several full courts, and you usually had to wait your turn to play. We had never lost.

Once, we walked up a flight of stairs to an older court. There we were to play five large, athletic looking men. They averaged five inches above us. They also could leap higher and run faster.

Penetrating their defense was near impossible, so we stuck to our strengths. Our center stayed inside and fought for every loose ball. Michael played his power forward position, working hard inside, with impeccable passing skills. Our point guard flawlessly protected and moved the ball. Myself, as the shooting guard, and our other forward were very similar. We possessed good court sense, and were excellent shooters with a quick release. Often, the best shot we could get was me drilling a two-handed pass to the small forward, leading him towards the basket neck-high, so he'd catch the ball in his shooting motion. Even then, the giant guarding him would almost block his shot.

They were shooting leaping, twisting, show-off shots. We couldn't stop them from getting their shot off, but they didn't make a high percentage. We took an early lead, even though they were getting three shots to our one. They realized their error, and began playing normal ball, but it was too late. Though they scored each time down, so did we. We won. I heard later that our opponents were redshirted Indiana University players.

I got to read some of Rudi's fascinating book, *Spiritual Cannibalism*, while it was still in manuscript form in the Ashram.

On my journey to Majorca with Maharishi's followers, I had a layover of two hours in New York. Rudi owned an antique shop there. I had the shop's address, but no idea where it was, plus no knowledge of the local transportation. I didn't even know if Rudi would be there, but I had to check—just in case. Walking out of the airport, I asked the first person I ran into if he knew how to get to Rudi's address. He pointed to a nearby bus that was just pulling up, saying, "That bus will take you there." I got off where the driver suggested, and again asked directions from the first person I ran into. He told me that Rudi's was around the next corner, so, in a remarkably short ten minutes after my plane landed I was close to Rudi's.

I walked around the corner, up to the door, stop and look in. Antiques are arranged artistically, even when in piles. There are no people in sight. I open the door. A thick blissful air immediately engulfs me … I willfully force myself in … I'm in another dimension …

time stops. I have no need to move or to understand. I see Rudi sitting in the back. I walk up to him, but am incapable of speech, unless he speaks first.

Rudi says, "How are you?"

I tell him of my planned trip to Majorca.

He says, "The problem with Maharishi's meditation is that it doesn't go far enough."

Months later, Maharishi says that Kundalini Yoga is too powerful, dangerous. Much later, I reflect on these statements. Both teachers are highly evolved. They just do what they individually need, to contact their soul and stabilize that contact.

A customer comes in. Rudi goes to speak to her. I busy myself, looking in a pile of ink drawings by Zen masters. Each drawing tells a story, a parable. I'm enthralled by each parable's timeless wisdom. I intuitively know what each means, as clearly as if the artist is speaking directly to me.

The lady leaves. Rudi starts doing some work. It is time for me to go. I leave, to fulfill my promise, though at this time, I want to stay.

Once, while in Majorca, I had four days off. I spent them in a cave, hidden amongst the rocks, next to a small beach. I wanted to find out how Rudi's and Maharishi's techniques compared. The morning sun would wake me, and then I'd bathe in the sea. I had fruit for breakfast. The rest of the day, I'd spend in meditation. I'd alternate the meditations, but there came a point when they were indistinguishable. I became so hypersensitive that I'd physically feel waves of sharp tension coming from anyone who would come within twenty feet. At the end of the four days it was very difficult to leave my cave.

Once, while in Fiuggi, I again practiced both techniques, though this time it came spontaneous. I was sitting on a bench in a hotel courtyard. I blanked out. When I came to, I had no memory. I knew I was a man, and all that entailed; but, I had no name, no past, and no personality. I didn't know where I was. It was freeing, fresh, but some worry came in. The thought quickly came, that I should find music.

I walked out of the garden. There was a faint, far-off sound, that I could feel not hear. I followed it to a jukebox. Standing in front of the jukebox, the blissful sounds were like nectar, easily returning my memory.

Rudi died in a plane crash on February 21, 1973. I heard that he predicted it. I heard that he didn't die from the crash, but exploded from the inside … that everyone else lived. Could it be that Rudi absorbed all the tension, so that others would live?

A few times, when I felt the people were ready, and the conditions were right, I'd pass on Rudi's Technique. The first time, it was nearly spontaneous, as it fit into a class I was teaching that had an unusually high number of advanced students. I wanted the exactness to be respected. Once, when doing the technique while my eyes were closed, I saw an outline of Rudi, filled in, in white. The white felt clearly to be the presence of Swami Nityananda. This was years after both had left their physical bodies.

Another time, while teaching, I told a story about Swami Nityananda to illustrate the compassion of the high souls. In this story, in Mangalore, India, Nityananda had a lady devotee whose husband didn't understand her devotion to the Master. In a fit of rage, the husband beats his wife. She is lashed with a belt until blood is drawn. In a few days, the devotee again sees Nityananda and tells of her beating. Nityananda replies, "You got the lash but who got the pain? See." With this, Nityananda shows her his back, which has the exact marks as her lashing. As I am telling this story, I'm so overwhelmed by the depth of Nityananda's compassion that I must stop speaking and turn my head away, to stop a flood of tears.

I've only seen Swami Chetanananda once since Rudi died. At that time, Swami Chetanananda's physical presence was extremely powerful.

Swami Chetanananda and his organization have produced some wonderful books and tapes that I'm continuously learning from.

It's clear to me that when people at a young age learn that they are not limited by their environmental circumstances, and are taught techniques (like Rudi's) to transcend the external, that they have a high probability of accomplishing more in life.

Here are a few examples of what Rudi's students have accomplished. Steven Ott became Swami Khecaranatha. Dean Gitter became a successful businessman and music producer. He produced Odetta's debut album, *Odetta Sings Ballads and Blues*. John Mann wrote an insightful book on his time with Rudi. Bruce Joel Rubin won the Academy Award for Best Original Screenplay for *Ghost*. And Jesse Slokum wrote informative and creative Internet articles while calling himself "*Court Jester to the Empire of the Spirit*." When our inner energies are strong and moving, and we surrender to a higher potential, anything is possible.

Years later, in Bloomington, I went to what had been the ashram restaurant on 10th Street, to see if any old devotees still worked there—it was still a restaurant. They called the one person they knew, and I waited in the parking lot. I saw her coming from a distance. As she got closer, I saw that she was heavy. Then I noticed her dull, frumpy cloths. Then that she was pale with a large nose. But after we spoke for ten minutes, I more accurately saw her as one of the most beautiful women I'd ever met.

On February 8, 2006, I was googling on a library computer and threw in Rudi's name. I was surprised that a lot came up—including a talk that Rudi gave on June 7, 1972. I made a printout of the talk to take home and savor at my leisure. When calmly reading it at home, I was stunned and pleased when I noticed that I was thinking it in Rudi's voice.

Yogi Bhajan was also taught a technique similar to Rudi's. Yogi Bhajan was told that this simple technique was all that was needed—that the previous complications were only because he wasn't ready.

Recently, I've been passing Rudi's Technique on more often. People do mention how much they like it, and I do grow each time I pass it on.

Chapter Eight: Pir Vilayat Khan, the Sufi Master

While living in Ann Arbor, Michigan, in 1977, I met some Sufis (Islamic Mystics). They were followers of Pir Vilayat Khan. The Sufis follow the true spiritual teachings of all religions. While I was living with them the Master came to nearby Detroit.

The lecture hall had about five hundred people. I sat close to the stage and about fifteen feet to Pir Vilayat's left. Pir's an older, thin man with a long beard. He spoke nervously. His eyes weren't clear. I was disappointed but listened anyway, out of respect, and hoping there would be some hidden jewels of wisdom. As he spoke, I became increasingly impressed by his incredible intellect and sensitivity. He was like the grandfather everyone wants. His nervousness gone, he weaved a timeless guided meditation. He took us to our inner purity.

Once, early in the lecture, Pir looked directly at me and said, "Fasting and doing mantras for forty days can do wonders." I asked some people after the lecture if they thought that Pir was looking specifically at me when he said that. They said that he was. I had already fasted often, but only for short periods. Inspired by Pir's advice, I read everything available and built up slowly, for seven years, and then fasted for forty days. I'd use cleansing food before and after, and juices during. During the forty-day fast, I meditated on each of the ninety-nine names of Allah. I became aware that just by thinking these names my consciousness and even the consciousness of those close to me could be changed. I also became aware that negativity is caused by a weakness in us that allows it to penetrate, that we are ultimately, totally, responsible for our individual reality.

I met my second wife, Arifa, in Ann Arbor. She was a Sufi. We wound up living in Lawrence, Kansas.

While in Lawrence, I had a vision of Hazrat Inayat Khan, Pir's father and spiritual guide. In the vision, I was in a photo lab. In the dark, I'm trying to thread a roll of film onto a wire frame, so the film can be developed. It's frustrating, tedious work. I crinkle the film—so it doesn't fit. I become angry, give up, and walk out into the light. You can see the images for a few seconds, before they fade. One is very clear, and in color—I usually only dream in black-and-white. It's a group photo of Hazrat and his followers, twenty-six altogether. I feel it to be in France in the 1920's. The color and details are flawless. It lasts for only a few seconds and then dissolves. Several weeks later, I see this same photo in the Sufi magazine, *The Message*; but the photo in *The Message* is only in black-and-white.

In the same vision, on the film, I see one other photo. This one is of three long-haired men sitting in a close circle, in meditation. The photo is from the vantage point of an unseen fourth meditator. The clarity and angle are as if I am actually there.

Pir Vilayat came to Lawrence while I was there. There was a lecture, and then a possibility of personal audience. I waited in the living room with the others, my name on the list of those seeking audience. It was a bad time for me. My family and job were falling apart. I was being tested and failing. My judgment was at an all time low.

My turn came. I didn't know what to expect, didn't know how to behave, and wasn't sure if I was worthy of even being there. I was told to just go in. I self-consciously push the door open. Pir is sitting on a cushion to my left. The room is dimly lit and empty of furniture. There's another cushion directly in front of Pir. Just as I'm deducing that I am supposed to sit there, Pir points to the empty cushion. My body effortlessly floats there and I sit ... I'm very comfortable. Although I have problems, I have no words worthy of breaking the exquisite silence. Pir speaks and I listen. He tells me of *Ya Azim*, the greeting that Sufi Masters greet each other with. It is the divinity that we all are a part of, which transcends individual differences. I relax deeper. My consciousness floats upward, out of the body, is rising still. I'm allowing it to continue. Suddenly I'm back in the body. It feels like Pir has pulled me back. The audience is over. I have to leave.

My marriage ended; again it was mainly my fault.

I reached Arifa by phone many years later. We still e-mail and occasionally write or talk on the phone. She lives a very honorable life in Oregon, organizing music concerts and cooperating with others on environmental projects.

In June of 2004, I woke with a powerful dream. In the dream,

I'm in a side room that's used for storage—mostly books. Some of the books are in color and luminous—one in particular grabs my attention. When the dream fads, I immediately go to the room, and pick up the book from my dream. It's a Sufi book I had forgotten about. Thumbing through it, I find a walking meditation for the mantra that Pir gave me. I had been looking for this for years. Several weeks later, I found out that this was around the time that Pir passed.

Pir Vilayat Khan is our spiritual elder.

Chapter Nine: Swami Amar Jyoti, the Swami of Light

Swami Amar Jyoti came to Evansville at the invitation of an old friend. The gatherings were small and mainly intellectual, low energy, even dull.

I had the opportunity to go to Swamiji's retreat at his Sacred Mountain Ashram in the mountains outside Boulder, Colorado. The low-key sessions in Evansville left me with small expectations—just a week of relaxation with wonderful scenery.

I pitched my tent away from the main buildings, so I could be quiet and free, participate in what appealed to me, and just do my separate meditations. I went to sleep with the sun and would wake naturally, before everyone else. I'd bathe, meditate, and wait for the others to get up.

One morning, I went to a small ledge to perform a sequence for attuning to the rising sun. I had practiced the sequence several times before, with minimal results. This time, though, as the first rays came I could feel them physically penetrate and energize my spine. It was very blissful. I was barely aware of the outer body.

After the sequence, I walked consciously to the morning meeting, chanting spontaneously. The body was light and felt luminous. I couldn't feel my feet touch the ground, but wasn't interested enough to look and see if they were.

Swami Jyoti's presence was powerful, here. Everyone was respectful and the music was divine.

Once, in the dining room, Swamiji walks by my table. Everyone stands in respect. My hands are folded in prayer pose. Swamiji embraces my hands. Warm blissful energy flows in my hands and feet, engulfing my whole body. It stays for about one, very-long minute.

I could see auras, for several days, as clearly as I ever have—wonderful colored lights outlining people's bodies, more vivid than rainbows, pleasing just to watch.

Sometimes I could tell where Swamiji was going or what he was going to say next.

The lecture sequence is of incredible depth and insight, particularly the conclusion. In this last lecture, Swamiji says that the ultimate is to simply look at our perfection and stop fighting with our illusion of limitations. Swamiji suggests thinking, "I am bliss/joy. I always have been bliss/joy. I always will be bliss/joy." Bliss works better for me. These are just words to help get in touch with the feeling. "*Remembering Yoga*", Swamiji calls it. I feel myself transcending when I first try this technique.

During one of the breaks, I went to a nearby home with some of the local devotees. They had hash oil. I had never had that, so smoked some with them. Back at the retreat, I no longer saw auras or knew what Swamiji Jyoti would do next. This smoking had been a big mistake, as getting high on hash oil had actually destroyed my much greater natural high.

Years later, after my mother's death, I was looking through her files. I found one on me. Inside was a newspaper photo of one of Swami Jyoti's lectures in Evansville. I had never seen this photo. In it Swamiji is looking directly at me. I remember that exact moment. At that time, I am opening to Swamiji … he gives me so much energy that I have to then leave the room, fearful I will explode in the cramped spaces.

Chapter Ten: Yogi Bhajan, the Great Yogi

As I mentioned towards the end of chapter three, **I first saw Yogiji** (Siri Singh Sahib Bhai Sahib Harbhajan Singh Khalsa) **in 1971 at a rock festival in Southern Louisiana.**

In 1975, I was in the bookstore of the University of Evansville. Thumbing through a book about new age groups, I spot a small photo of Yogiji. The photo becomes very clear … and everything else disappears from my sight. I then read what little is said of Yogiji. There's a gathering starting soon **in the mountains of New Mexico.** I know that I am supposed to go there.

I called the number listed, and made arrangements to meet others in St. Louis, and share expenses from there.

My traveling companions told me not to expect much—that forty days after the gathering (**Summer Solstice of 1975**) I'd notice some small changes.

We stopped briefly in Kansas City. The calm strength of the Kansas City Ashram still gives me a warm feeling, just remembering it.

There were some 1,500 people at the solstice site. We camped in tents. A clear mountain stream rolled next to the site.

My first White Tantric Yoga began with low expectations. We were meticulously lined up in rows of two, male and female facing each other—most were dressed in white and wearing turbans.

White Tantra is the purity of group energy. Red Tantra is the pure energy of one couple. Black Tantra is that same energy channeled in destructive ways.

Yogiji gave us a mantra to use and a physical position to hold. After a few minutes, I'm suddenly above the others … some hundred yards in the air … I have no body … yet I can see. Fear comes in. I hear Yogiji's voice, gently, clearly guiding me, just a few feet in front of me. He says, "Think the mantra." I do so, and I'm immediately back in my body.

Another time the Tantra was interrupted by a thunder storm. We were told to go into the nearest tent. I was in a tent with four or five others. I hadn't met any of them. They are bright and clear, like in a surrealistic painting. Just looking at them, I intuitively know a lot about them. It is too intense ... I just look at the floor, until the rain stops.

Once, walking through small woods that ran parallel with the stream, I happened upon Yogiji with about ten others, including several children. Respectfully, I sit down. The atmosphere is energized, yet calm. Brief words are spoken by a few others, including Yogiji, but the wonderful silence is much more prevalent. An hour or so later, Yogiji stands, then the rest of us leave in unison—the group disperses.

Between scheduled events, I was walking behind the stage. Approaching one end of the stage, I hear this wonderful singing ... I'm drawn in. Looking around the corner, I see several hundred ladies chanting the *Adi Shakti Mantra*. Waves of bliss float into me. It comes to me that this gathering is probably just for the ladies. As I'm self-consciously turning to leave, Bibiji (Yogiji's wife) turns gracefully, looks at me and smiles. I walk away full and happy.

There were competitive games, lectures, learning groups, and incredible vibrancy and strength—everywhere—much more useful knowledge than I was capable of absorbing.

Once, I went to a group martial arts class. About fifty of us were in a circle with the leader, Pink Krishna, in the center. Krishna had her back to me. I started to imagine that I was attacking her—with no real intent to do so. She immediately turned and looked directly in my eyes.

At night there was music and speakers of various paths. The days were warm, but as the sun dropped the temperature plunged. Once I was caught listening in my day clothes as the sun faded. Not wanting to miss anything, I relaxed my cold extremities, breathed deep into the spine, felt the warmth radiating, and stayed for hours without feeling cold.

Every moment was of an essence that I was sure was the way things were meant to be. The discipline was extreme, getting up hours before the sun, cold showers, hard exercise, and moral teachings.

The path of Yogiji, the Sikhs, is an outward perfection that when done fully leads to the inner perfection, or so it seems to me. The Hindu path is an inward perfection that when done fully leads to the outer perfection, though it's really not this simplistic … for outer and inner, are ultimately, the same.

I left the solstice with books and tapes, to study, enjoy, and practice from. I still use them, and newer ones.

In December of 1975, I went to my first Winter Solstice in Florida. There were about a third as many participants, with a much larger proportion of the more dedicated *yogis*. The overall energy was more inward and calm.

The first morning, I was awakened by the wonderful music of a strolling guitarist playing and singing a gentle, inspiring, wake-up song—at first I thought it was a dream.

There was an orange and grapefruit grove next to the Tantric site. The oranges were sweet and delicious. The grapefruits were even sweet, and very large, too big to eat a whole one in one sitting.

The Tantras usually started much later than scheduled. Often, when they ran late, some dance music would be played. People would dance away their tensions—healthy, young, and expressive people. On one such occasion, I was late to the Tantric. As I approached, I saw the people dancing.

About a hundred yards in front of me, there was one lady that stuck out, with graceful precision spins in perfect time to the music. I live to dance, and, of course, thought it would be great to dance with her, but the people weren't dancing with partners. This being a spiritual gathering, it seemed inappropriate to try and be her dance partner. I was, kind of, hoping she'd be ugly, so it would be easier to forget her; but the closer I got the more beautiful she became. Her face and figure were perfection. Her movements, close up, were even more graceful.

I fade into the crowd and allow the transforming, musical environment to move me. I am happy, in my element, and in a few minutes, I have forgotten her … tensions and desires have dissolved. I am one with the dance.

Like in a dream, she is now facing me. We move energetically to the same music and thus to each other. We communicate through movement … I adjust to her style … she dances my way … our styles merge. We continue for what seems like hours. After the dancing, she tells me, "You have tremendous energy."

We were supposed to be in silence for several days, so spoke, usually, through writing. I'll call her the Dancing Sikh. We ate meals together, were Tantric partners, and went for walks, mostly in silence.

Near the end of the gathering, I went to Yogiji to ask for a spiritual name. Not knowing if I was worthy, I went after the stated closing time. There were still a few people in line. I took my place in the back of the line. The gate was shut behind me.

When my turn came, I walked up the back steps, through the screened-in porch, and into a room with Yogiji and two secretaries. The air is thick and energized. I want to talk for a long time, so I can extend my stay, but it's impossible to find a problem large enough to merit breaking the silence.

I hand Yogiji a card with my name, address, birthday, and which ashram I want to live in. Yogiji takes the card, writes on it, and hands it to me, saying, "Guru Dyal Singh. It means mercifully compassionate." I ask him to repeat it and closely watch and listen as he forms the words. I want to get it right. I had heard of some who didn't get their spiritual names right the first time and never got a second chance. After several repetitions, Yogiji states sharply, "That's enough!" I leave at a normal pace. Since then, I've mostly used just the Dyal part. The rest can lead to many complications, or maybe I'm just too weak.

I walk out the gate and sit under a large tree, some ten yards away—feeling the subtleties of my precious spiritual name. Yogiji has said that our spiritual names are the nature our highest destiny is meant to manifest.

The Dancing Sikh is walking by. She sits beside me and we discuss our spiritual names. There is a tangible purity between us, as if we are both thirteen again … at one point, I notice that my hand is on her knee.

I had to leave the gathering abruptly, as my ride left without notice. I searched quickly to say goodbye to the Dancing Sikh—finding her eating. It was very awkward. She was still married, although she said that she was getting a divorce. Others were listening—she wanted details on when we would meet again. I told her I'd see her at future gatherings, which I really thought would happen.

I sent her a birthday card, with my return address, to where I thought she lived. My finances became worse. I went to all the gatherings I could afford, but I never saw her again.

At one of the low points in my life, several years later, when I could think of nothing worth living for, I remembered her name. The ugliness went away immediately. I could not think of her and anything negative at the same time.

I believe other Sikh ladies have the same name. Once, I read a poem under her name. If it was her, I could see at what point in the poem I came into her life.

In 1977, I attended another Winter Solstice on the same site. I made many new friends and saw some old ones. Everyone seemed to be worth knowing—the best of people.

I had a shoulder that was hurting. One of the more experienced Yogis showed me an exercise for it. I went off by myself to practice it— the arm of the injured shoulder in the air, and the other arm down. I practiced for the required time. Powerful energy was moving through my outstretched arm. I quit the exercise and dropped my arm ... the arm stayed in the air! I had to *pull* the outstretched arm down with my other hand.

During one of the Tantric waiting periods when no music was played, the tension level was unusually high. There were three oranges beside me. I picked up the oranges, stood up, and began to juggle. Some around me gave disapproving glances, while others stretched and relaxed. The overall tension level seemed to decrease.

After one of the Tantric sessions I felt unusually tense. I relaxed, hoping a solution would come. My body moved on its own ... first stretching ... then the hands went to the eyes, moving consciously down, taking heat and tension away. I looked around. Two ladies, some thirty yards away, caught my attention. They had a beautiful purple light, about six inches thick, around their heads and shoulders. Their light seemed more real than the body and very pleasing to the eyes. This was the first time I'd clearly seen auras, although, I had been able to feel them for a long time.

Auras are the magnetic fields of the body. The polarity between male and female is what builds our magnetic fields, and gives us strength and protection from diseases and negativity. The strongest, natural, positive, creative use of this energy is the White Tantric Yoga of Yogi Bhajan. Ninety percent of our sexual energy is meant to be reabsorbed into the spine. It then travels up the spine to activate our higher brain functions. When we have normal sex our deep psyche merges with the other. If we are with more than one person, we are pulled in different directions, and forced to remain only on the superficial.

The nights of the Tantric days were rich with incredibly talented and creative musicians—using both English and the Mantras of the Sikhs. One of the guitarists was Vikram Singh Khalsa, who was Vic Briggs when he played with the rock group *The Animals*.

Sometimes during the Tantric exercises, Yogiji would have people drop out completely once they had to drop their hands. Individual exercises could last as long as an hour. Several times, I was the last one to drop. A few people came up to me and said that it was thought that I would be Yogiji's successor. Reflecting on this, years later, I think I could have gone much further, but not that far.

Several years later, I was traveling in the Detroit area. I dropped by the Sikh Ashram in the Detroit suburb of Beverly Hills, and wound up living there for two months.

I worked hard at the ashram, but unsuccessfully looked for outside work.

After several weeks I was seeing auras daily, particularly during morning *Sadhana* (spiritual practices). The instructor's aura was often larger than anyone else's, but only when he was teaching.

After one sadhana session, one of the ashram guitarists was spontaneously playing for one of the stragglers. I went downstairs to get my harmonica. Sometimes I play good, sometimes not. This time I relaxed into the pure environment and quality guitarist. Wonderful improvisations came from my harmonica. After we finished playing, the straggler asked me incredulously, "How'd you do that?" I couldn't explain. I've had a few good sessions before and after, but none near the quality of that day.

I got along with most of the *Sangeet* (seekers of truth). Unfortunately, one I didn't get along with was the acting leader. Usually the sadhana was when I got my juice for the rest of the day, but when he led it I was getting progressively worsening headaches. It reached a crescendo where I could do nothing but prepare for the next sadhana.

One morning the headache was unbearable. I surrendered deeper. Surrendering deeper always brings a solution. We were chanting. As I surrendered, my head went to the floor on its own. The headache immediately stopped! The leader yelled at me to sit up. I sat up immediately. He continued talking in harsh tones. I physically felt his words strike me. My body recoiled and yelled the mantra back at him. I got up, walked downstairs, packed, and left.

Looking back on my experiences, I realize I was lucky, made many mistakes, had some courage, some discernment; but it wasn't until the 1990's that I really matured enough to appreciate and utilize what I'd learned.

Sometime after living in Detroit, I'm in Evansville and writing a lady in D.C. I get a chance to go briefly **to Atlanta, where Yogiji is**, before heading up the coast to see her.

We pull into a dead end street. The Ashram consists of several average-looking, suburban homes. I can only stay a few hours—don't know if I'll get to see Yogiji. Ten to twelve people are walking around, most towards the same house. I join them, walk in the door, take off my shoes, and step into the living room. Some sixty people are sitting knee-to-knee on the floor. I find a small space, out of the flow of traffic, and sit.

Yogiji is some eighteen feet in front of me. He's sitting in an easy chair, very busy, directing, answering, asking, eating, occasionally speaking to the group.

I'm thinking, "I'll have to leave soon."

Yogiji looks directly at me and says, "If you can't live gracefully, it's best to die gracefully—right!"

I reflect a few seconds and say, "Right."

I can only stay for a few more minutes—I don't understand why Yogiji spoke those words to me.

I leave for D.C. I'm hitchhiking through a big city, late at night. Suddenly, it's very cold. The darkness sneaks in. I'm hungry, my backpack's heavy. I look for a place to rest—all around are taverns and black men. I see a church yard, with bushes to hide behind. Once nestled behind the bushes, some drunks come and sit on the other side. They don't see me. Their talk is crude and angry. I'm afraid to sleep or move. It gets colder. In the morning the men leave.

I continue walking down the highway. My back and knees hurt. I'm obsessed with uncharacteristic negative thoughts. I surrender, so a solution can come. The body goes to the side, and I'm guided to do the Sikh meditation *"Meditation to Totally Recharge You"*. My physical strength and mental calm are totally restored. I continue on.

Later, the trip again becomes unpleasant. I arrive with a headache.

My friend is different, more distant. Her friends don't like me. We're walking by a construction site, arguing. There's a plywood fence around the site. My anger is boiling over. I kick the plywood. Unfortunately, there's a solid (4x4) behind the spot I kick—bad pain! Now, my big toe is swollen, and I walk with a painful limp.

There's time to reflect. I'm having trouble finding work. I'm in the house. She's gone. Her sister's there. The tension's thick. I'm again getting obsessed with hateful thoughts. Yogiji's words come clearly, "If you can't live gracefully, it's best to die gracefully—right!" Those words pull me out. I left the next morning.

It's 1982, and I'm back in Evansville—there's not much positive reinforcement. I'm thinking, "If Yogiji is really my teacher, I should open up to him." I write him an honest and respectful letter, not knowing what, if anything, to expect. An answer comes quickly. The letter has a physical presence, as if Yogiji's with me. He answers deeper than my questions and comments. We continue writing. Each letter I receive is a blessing. Even when writing I feel a blessing, an opening, clarifying, tangible energy.

One letter I sent Yogiji was about my little nephew Kevin's seizures. The seizures were getting progressively worse. All the other relatives wanted to get him doped up. The morning after mailing this letter, it came to me in meditation to have Kevin do a specific meditation.

In this technique, you sit straight with the arms out to the sides just enough to feel tension, but not touching anything. You inhale through the nose taking the awareness from the top of the head to the throat. Then exhale through the nose taking the awareness down the shoulders, arms, and off the finger tips. Next, start the inhale from the feet to the throat, and you exhale as before. Eyes are closed throughout. If you feel heaviness in the hands, you can shake them a little. No time limit, but do it regularly.

Kevin came over a few hours later. I'm aware, as a separate observer, that he's being shown the technique. To my surprise he does it, and feels it working immediately. Kevin was about ten then and is thirty-four now ... the seizures have not returned. I heard years later, that when writing Yogiji the answer can come in the morning meditation. I've passed this technique on to many people (a neighbor lady was also healed by it), but, so far, the medical profession isn't interested in it. I call it *Kevin's Technique*.

Friday, September 28, 1984, I went to a Tantric in St. Louis. I got to stay in the home of one of the students, and met interesting, creative, and good people.

I volunteered for work (*seva*), which is the normal thing to do, and received a blessing while doing it.

I'm inside the Ashram, vacuuming hard-to-reach steps. Clearly to my mind, come some of the words from one of theSikh teachers: Hearing that the Lord can give me refuge, I sought His shelter; I have sought His Mercy, that I might be united with Him. As I murmured His sweet Name, in the company of the holy, my antipathies ceased, and I became the dust of all men's feet.

My labor is turned to joy. The meanings of the words are alive to me.

Saturday was the day of the Tantric. The whole day was full, varied, rich, challenging, and uplifting. Our higher natures were emerging.

Sunday morning is the Gurdwara, the Sikh church service—there's chanting, scripture reading and interpretation, respect, and peace. Yogiji humbles himself before the Siri Guru Granth Sahib (the Sikh scriptures, which are considered the living Guru). Yogiji twitches uneasily. This is the first time I've seen him as having an ordinary human weakness; yet, I respect him even more, because it makes his accomplishments seem greater, by comparison. Great men are not different from us, but our own highest potential. Was he just a spark from the scriptures? How vast these scriptures must be.

On the bus, on the way home, I'm writing by a dim light. My inner being is awakened. Poems are coming out. I'm suddenly aware that the thoughts inside me are in Yogiji's voice. I'm frightened. I instinctively become so concentrated on my environment that all thoughts stop. One of the poems written on this bus ride is:

Gracious Lord

I wanted a fairy tale—
    for my Lord to come in a flash of light,
    but He had compassion on me
    and granted me hard work.
I hoped in drowsy reverie
    the Lord would make me great,
    but He had compassion on me
    and made me a servant to all.
I wished that all my worldly needs
    would come like a soft, cool breeze,
    but He had compassion on me
    and gave me pain as a guide.
I prayed my Lord
    would bring me worldly wealth and fame,
    but he had compassion on me
    and granted me His Name.
I sit here knowing I have been unworthy,
    but my Gracious Lord
        has never left
        my side.

In November, 1985, I went to another Tantric in Columbus, Ohio. Jagan Nath Singh came from St. Louis to Evansville, and we traveled together the rest of the way. We shared a hotel room with Sat Singh, a friend from Winter Solstice, and Guru Charan Singh, who I lived with in the Detroit Ashram. We all shared a light, positive, honest approach to life. We hung out together, went to the hotel sauna, and shared stories and jokes.

The Tantric, as always, brought increased energy and insight.

Back in Evansville, on the return trip, Jagan Nath kindly volunteered to play has electric violin for my ailing mother. It was a fine blessing for her.

July 19–20, 1986, I was at the opening of Swami Satchidananda's Lotus Shrine in Virginia. The festivities were attended by about five thousand people.

While at registration, Yogi Bhajan and his entourage walked past me. I felt self-conscious because I wasn't wearing a turban.

Later, after a lengthy and inspiring auditorium program, I walk nervously to the front, where Yogiji had been sitting. Drifting through the crowd, I come to a small opening to an empty circle about ten yards in diameter. Yogiji and I are at opposite points on the circle. I'm gently pulled to him. We exchange a few words, touch hands, and then I leave, feeling strong and clear.

Many other spiritual leaders and celebrities were there. I got high, just by walking close to Wallace Black Elk, Grace Spotted Eagle, and their followers. Singer Carole King was also there.

In September of 1988, I went to another Tantric in St. Louis. This was the only one I went to that Yogiji wasn't there in person. It was done through a video. I was in intense pain through most of it, maybe from my emerging back problems.

I started teaching Yoga shortly after I began to study it. Not because I felt ready to teach; but because, sometimes, I seemed a better option than what was available. Yogiji's techniques were usually the most functional for me to pass on, at least as the framework; because they brought fast results with minimal effort and with many of the other techniques, I often didn't have permission or the ability to teach them.

A friend, who teaches martial arts, brought me a student of his. The student was to be operated on for a collapsed lung. I taught him a sequence for expanding lung capacity ... he felt it work immediately. He practiced it regularly for several weeks, then went for one last exam before his operation ... they told him that he no longer needed the operation!

Each of the first twenty-seven letters from Yogiji (over an eight year period) came with a tangible physical energy. The twenty-eighth letter didn't have that presence. I was concerned. Had I lost my connection? What did I do wrong? I was surrendering deeper, searching for an answer, trying not to explode from worry.

While touching the letter, I happened to be thinking of Jean, one of my students. The energy returned. I told this to her, the next class she attended, as I'm handing her the letter. She took the letter silently, held it calmly for a few seconds, then looked at me and said. "It's alive."

Several months later, Jean casually mentioned that she has a daughter. The clear, strong thought came to me, "You don't know her well enough yet." I knew this to mean that I didn't know Jean well enough to talk to her about her daughter. I obeyed the words, but had no intellectual understanding of their meaning.

Soon Jean and I started dating. It only lasted for about six months. A few months after the breakup, I realized that the breakup had hurt the innocent child, so I asked Jean, "I would like to have visitation rights with Jesse?"

Jean answers, "All right, you treated her better than her father did."—but sadly, over the years, I lost contact with Jesse.

I'm continuously learning and practicing Yogiji's teachings, and passing on as much as I'm capable. The depth and range of his knowledge is, compared to our societal norms, vast.

In October of 2004, I was walking past the Sikh altar in my home. I hadn't used this altar much recently. I'm physically pulled to the altar. I sit down and put on the Ram Das Chant Tape. This is the chant that's done before the Yoga class starts. I had looked at it as just a preparatory relaxing and energizing chant. Yet this time, I get very clear images of people with the accompanying thought that I should avoid them. I act on these visions and they shortly prove to be correct, as I am removed from a potentially dangerous situation. Several weeks later, I found out that this was around the time that Yogiji passed, and that others had messages from Yogiji of a similar magnitude.

Yogiji has much of the knowledge we need, to consciously attune to our truest nature—here are some excerpts from letters I received from Yogiji:

…"Let prayer be your guide and companion to victory of soul."

…"Keep writing to me and let us feel the oneness of Almighty God."

…"You are but a speck in the Universe. But you are a part of it—and when you let the past die, and learn to embrace tomorrow, your heart will open, your soul will be uplifted and you will experience, feel and understand that connection with God. That is Truth and Truth is always yours.

Door remains open. Only the ego closes it out of pain of past and fear and mistrust of tomorrow. Keep the door open to your highest consciousness and inspire many to walk in with you."

…"Meditate on the *Nadh* or sound current of *Har* (the creative God) and all difficulties will he crossed."

…"Practice Kundalini Yoga, teach Kundalini Yoga, share its technology with all that they may learn to live in health, happiness and holiness."

…"Keep up. Keep in touch. A life of commitment and a life of sacrifice is a life of divinity."

…"Just remember, my son. You are the creator of your own experiences. When you give your head, and remember God within, the walls will seem small. Happiness is, understanding the God within. Time and space will test your grace, but as the *Dharmic* man you shall rise above to live in your excellence."

…"My love for you is forever. By the grace of Guru Ram Das together we shall walk this path to its righteous end."

…"You must understand that you have to be very real. It is time to phoenix yourself from the ashes of your past. You have not been living in the practical spiritual reality. The basic feeling in you must be the essence of Dharma. Understand who you are. Live in your grace, build, and crystallize the spirit in you. You have the greatest potential, and are my dear son. I will like you to honestly consider my words and let me know."

…"Love you. God and Guru have guided you to write the poem *Gracious Lord* as a confirmed moment to ecstasy."

…"Miracles happen. They just need to be recognized."

…"Love you very much. In the Name of the Cosmos which prevails through everyBODY and the Holy Nam which holds the world."

Chapter Eleven: the Dalai Lama, Ocean of Wisdom

In the mid-'80s I taught some Yoga in Bloomington, Indiana. One of the people I made friends with was Bea Farris. Bea invited me to visit her at her home. She said I would like the house she was renting a room in, and particularly would like her landlady, who she said I had a lot in common with.

The home sure was impressive—a three-story, colonial log home, with additions, including an outdoor hot tub. The owner, Cherry Merritt-Darriau, bought the home and her three grown sons moved it to forty acres of virgin forest she purchased seven miles east of Bloomington. When there is a booklet for the Bloomington Preservation Tour, her home is on the cover.

A winding, hilly, two-lane road slows you down until you reach a sign that says *Deer Path Yoga Center*. Cramped parking and a large friendly dog greet you as you turn in. A small garden, a wide, comfortable porch, and the freshest air possible, make you feel at home, even if it's your first time here.

Cherry is a certified Yoga Teacher under Swami Rama's Himalayan Institute. I haven't seen Swami Rama in person, but have learned a lot from his books. In Indiana, I rarely meet someone who has been into Yoga as long or deep as me, so it's like meeting a forgotten sister or brother. Cherry and I speak the same language, have similar assumptions on life, and know different pieces of the giant and mysterious jigsaw puzzle called Yoga.

On Cherry's land there are life-size sculptures of Cherry and her daughter, Andrea, by her ex-husband Jean-Paul Darriau. Jean-Paul was an art professor at Indiana University, and most, or all, of the sculptures in the city of Bloomington are his.

Cherry has a Masters Degree in Clinical Psychology, works at a mental hospital, and teaches Yoga and French at Indiana University— besides the Yoga she teaches at her home.

I saw Cherry twice more when visiting Bloomington. Once when I'm helping a friend from high school move; and once when my sister, Janet, and I, stop off on the way to her doctor's appointment in Indianapolis.

Then in 1987, I hear that the Dalai Lama is coming to Bloomington. There's a new Tibetan Cultural Center on 108 acres southeast of Bloomington, started by the Dalai Lama's older brother, Thubten J. Norbu, a retired Professor of Tibetan Studies at Indiana University.

I arrange to stay with Cherry. She graciously picks me up at the bus station.

September 24, 1987, Cherry and I go to the Tibetan Culture Center. We're on the land early, because Cherry is connected to the organizers. You could easily miss it, as it's hidden in the suburbs. From the road, all you can see are a few parked cars.

The Dalai Lama is here for the consecration of the Jangchub Chorten. It's a Tibetan style monument. The Chorten is thirty-five feet high, with a twenty-one foot square base, and one hundred tons of cement. Inside the Chorten are many holy relics. The monument, in its entirety, represents the path to enlightenment, as expressed by its height, reaching towards the heavens. I go up to the impressive white base and gold-topped monument, and read the inscription on the plaque in front of the Chorten:

In recent times, conflict and aggression throughout the world have visited death and destruction on countless innocent people. This has been especially true in Tibet, a land devoted to religion, where more than one million people have perished since 1950, when the Chinese Army occupied the country. Even now, as the devastating occupation continues, Tibetan lives are threatened, and the vast majority of Tibetan people are subject to policies whose ultimate aim is to bring an end to their way of life.

This Chorten stands before the people of the world who love justice and peace, as testimony to the miseries suffered by the Tibetan people and the justness of their cause. In that sense, it stands also as a memorial to all people who have similarly suffered. May it remain so for all times.

Our hopes as Tibetans and the hopes of people everywhere to dwell in nonviolence, peace, and security will together endure as inward supports for all our spirits.

To my right comes a small group of people walking slowly from behind the monument. In the front is a man, I somehow know, to be the Dalai Lama. I reflexively put my hands in prayer pose. As they come within a few feet of me, the Dalai Lama looks at me and giggles (at the time I was taking myself too seriously). He stops in front of me. I bow respectfully from the waist. His hands embrace mine for just a few seconds—he walks on. There's a strong blissful current running through my arms. It continues for several minutes. Only when it ends am I capable of separating my hands.

The next day, September 25, 1987, Bea Farris and I go to the official ceremonies. A newly constructed Ceremonial Pavilion is set up in the back of the property. We're on time, but there are several thousand people already seated. We're too far back to see, much less hear. There's a small road to the right that curves up to the stage. We walk on that road looking for an opening in the crowd where we can sit. Close to the stage, there's an empty, roped-off VIP area. I talk Bea into going into the VIP area, telling her that you can't look at us and tell that we're not VIPs. Shortly after we're seated, a large group of people come from behind the stage to sit with us. A short, thin, pale man with a very nice business suit sits next to Bea. The ceremony is a Long Life Offering to His Holiness the Fourteenth Dalai Lama. The energy is great, yet mostly in Tibetan. Occasionally someone comes next to me to shoot photos into our VIP area. Being a photographer, I sometimes give them exposure tips. Later, we find out that the man next to Bea was the actor, Richard Gere.

There's a lunch break, then the actual consecration ceremony on a smaller stage closer to the Chorten. It's uncomfortably crowded, but when we can walk around, there's a joyful energy.

That night there's a free public lecture in the Indiana University Auditorium. Here are some excerpts from the Dalai Lama's lecture: The most important thing is seeing someone as another human being. So I am talking on that level. At this moment, thinking on these lines, it can be easier to communicate. ◆ Sometimes it so happens that the means or the systems that we use to overcome our problems become problems by themselves. ◆ If you compare external factors and internal factors, the internal factors are more important, more effective. If you are not mentally happy, then despite having all the best surrounding you, you may not feel happy. On the opposite side, if you are mentally calm, satisfied, and happy, then even without external, material wealth, you may be alright. ♦ Anger destroys the best part of the human brain, that part which can judge between right and wrong. It is very important to analyze the actual situation. Only then can a counter measure be accepted, and even then without anger. ♦ Some people feel or regard tolerance and patience as a sign of weakness. I do not agree with this. If you have inner strength, then tolerance becomes possible. If deep down you feel some kind of weakness, then often you get irritated. So therefore, tolerance and patience are real signs of inner strength. ♦ There are two forms of nonviolence. The higher is to consider others as more important than oneself. The lower is to do no harm. This is the essence of Buddhism. ♦ There are some things that bring superficial pleasure, but bring pain in the long run—other things that bring temporary pain, but pleasure in the long run. What matters the most is the long run. ♦ The cause of pain is not understanding the actual nature of things, thus, right understanding can overcome pain. ♦ A good kind of ego says statements like, "I can do this. I can do that." ♦ Be thankful of those who put you in a situation where you need patience. Seeing problems from a greater distance can give you patience. Analyzing the negative can bring a solution, or make you realize there is no way to overcome, so no need to worry. ♦ I have some Christian friends that use Buddhist techniques. This is possible because all religions value being good, honest, and open-hearted. ♦ If you find some of my teachings useful, you can keep them. If not, you can forget them—no problem. ♦ Good motivation becomes positive. Bad motivation, even in something holy, becomes negative. ♦ Love without attachment is the highest. To see all as God's manifestation can lessen the pain of loss.

The next time the Dalai Lama came to Bloomington was July25–27, 1996. Again, I am blessed to be there, and again I stay with Cherry. There are a lot more people this time—probably, or at least partially, because His Holiness had won the Nobel Peace Prize in 1989. He gave two-thirds of the money to lepers in Lucknow. In 1991, Indiana Lieutenant Governor Frank O'Bannon added the Tibetan Cultural Center to the list of the Department of Tourism's "Hidden Treasures of Indiana."

There is to be a groundbreaking ceremony for the *Chamtse Ling*

Temple (as named by the Dalai Lama)—it means "Realm of Love and Kindness". As part of the groundbreaking and cornerstone ceremony, the Dalai Lama will give a teaching and perform the ritual for *Aspirational Bodhicitta.*

Friday night, July 26, 1996, Cherry, Shehira Davezac, and I, go to a free lecture at Indiana University Auditorium. Shehira is from Egypt and teaches History of Oriental Art at IU. We stop off for tea on Shehira's patio before going to the lecture. Shehira tells fascinating stories of growing up in Egypt. Her family, and others she knew, had the easy Darshan of Muslim mystics. Shehira has a keen intellect that quickly points out illogical statements—I like it.

On the way to the auditorium, we stop off at a large health food store—there, I see two people from Evansville, Jann Thomas and Maria Venturini.

Waiting in line at the auditorium, I see two more people from Evansville, Jackie Freeman and Peggy Pruitt. I also see the actor Steven Seagal go in the VIP entrance. He looks like a giant, standing much taller than the relatively short Tibetans. The 3,700-seat auditorium fills quickly. Others have to view from the TV screens in the Fine Arts Auditorium, Woodburn Hall, or Indiana Memorial Union, or just watch the live TV coverage from someplace else.

Once in the auditorium, a wonderful bamboo flutist performs with great depth and sensitivity—sometimes, it seems as if he is playing several instruments at once. Everyone is respectful and attentive. During the Indiana University President's introductory remarks, the Dalai Lama bends over in his chair and playfully waves at some people in the audience. Here are some quotes from the Dalai Lama's lecture: Conflicts and differences are always there, like in a family, but taking a broader perspective can lessen the sting. ♦ Focus not on different techniques, but the underlying effectiveness in bringing about respect for and appreciation of others. ♦ Violence is outdated. ♦ Real compassion has respect. ♦ It's impossible to be a help to the world community without compassion. ♦ People of all walks of life must acknowledge their differences and celebrate their commonality. ♦ The supermarket of religions available today is a good thing given the diverse needs of people. ♦ The world is interconnected. Destroying your enemy is like destroying your own leg. ♦ I know that people can change—I was very short-tempered when young.

Back at Cherry's we are greeted by her cat, Larry, and dog, Bart. Bart is even mentioned in one of Dark Rain Thom's books, as Bart divorced his owners and came to live with Cherry.

Early the next morning, July 27, 1996, I went with Cherry to the Tibetan Cultural Center for the official groundbreaking ceremonies. I didn't have enough money to get in, so thought I would just wait on the outside, absorbing the good energy.

Cherry says that her intuition is that I can get in for free. We both know that sincere seekers are never turned away. Technically this may be true, but since I'm not famous or a clear representative of a recognized tradition, I doubt if they'll let me in. The young girl at registration says I have to pay. Cherry still thinks I can get in for free. To satisfy her, while she is registering, I walk up to the guarded entrance—thinking they'll just say no, and I can leave. Two armed policemen and two Tibetan men stand at the entrance. I walk up to the policemen and humbly say, "I have no money, but would like to come in." The Tibetans are standing about five yards to my right. One of them waves me over. Then one picks a ticket out of his pocket and says, "Today is your lucky day. Someone just gave me this ticket." He asks my name, I tell him. He asks for some ID. I show him my driver's license. I'm now aware that they are checking me out. Both then politely introduce themselves and we shake hands. One asks where I'm from. I say, "Evansville." Now they are respectful and we are like brothers. I'm feeling a strong natural high, and just want to stay here and continue our dialogue. At this moment, Cherry walks up, I show her my ticket, and we walk into the ceremony site. Cherry says, "I see you met the Dalai Lama's nephews." Years later, Cherry's version is that I just boldly walk up to the entrance.

Inside, at the center's pavilion, the Dalai Lama's older brother, retired professor Thubten Norbu, spoke. He said that in 1906 in his previous incarnation as Tsutum Jigme Gyatso, he had accompanied the Thirteenth Dalai Lama to visit an important retreat center. On the way, they stopped in the village of Takster. There the Thirteenth Dalai Lama remarked of the loveliness of one particular home. This is the home in which the Fourteenth Dalai Lama was born, and Professor Norbu was born as his older brother. Professor Norbu says, "This gathering today, together with you, Your Holiness, is something which doesn't even come to pass in dreams."

The Dalai Lama then gave a teaching and performed the ritual for *Aspirational Bodhicitta*. There were several points that deeply affected me. One was when His Holiness said that individual enlightenment is selfish, plus you only have your own resources. But when you work for everyone's enlightenment you have all their accumulated resources. At that moment I felt a rush of energy, as if a previously unknown flood-gate was opened. Another insight was when he said that phenomena do not exist in their own right. They are all *dependent arising*, thus empty. My last insight was from the Dalai Lama's statement that realizing the inherent emptiness of phenomena is true wisdom ... and that through this wisdom our defilements can be removed and the true luminous and knowing nature of our minds can be revealed.

Looking through my old notes of that day, another point finally sinks in: the assumption of the existence of phenomena draws us into actions that contaminate—create *karma*.

I get to stay over a few more days with Cherry to accompany her and her old friend, John Hicks, to Chicago. We are going to the Guru Purnima (full moon celebration) of her guru, Swami Rama.

It is wonderful to enjoy the spiritual richness of Cherry's home. There are books, tapes, and walks—eating healthy food in her colonial/modern kitchen—visiting the hippies who she sold a little of her land to—just sitting on the porch, taking deep breaths, petting the dog and cat. The hippie children show me the fossils that rest in the small stream at the bottom of Cherry's property.

We drove to Chicago; Swami Rama wasn't there in person. The head man there was Pandit Dabral. Pandit Dabral had heard that I'd studied with some Sikhs. He started to be negative to me. I interrupted him saying I was a Bhakti (worship) Yogi. This slowed him some. Then I mentioned Sri Ganapati Sachchidananda Swamiji. He calmly, and even respectfully, said, "I've heard of him." Sri Ganapati Sachchidananda Swamiji is chapter fourteen.

The ritual there was that for a twenty-four hour period at least one person had to be meditating in their meditation room. I wound up being the only one in the meditation room for about ten of the twenty-four hours.

After this period is over, we all gather in the lecture hall. Sitting in the crowded room, I can barely stay awake. There appears before me a vision of Swami Rama's head—it's about twenty feet high and six feet wide. It only stays for a few seconds, but is very clear. I look around, and it doesn't seem, as though, anyone else sees him.

We drove through the night back to Bloomington.

Later that day, I had a little free time in Bloomington before my bus left. I went to the Snow Lion Restaurant and asked if one of the Dalai Lama's nephews was there. Then a husky Tibetan man came out and questioned me (it came to me later that he was probably a body guard). Then the nephew came out. We had a short, pleasant conversation, and then I left to catch my bus.

In 1999 the Dalai Lama came back to Bloomington. I try and open others to the spiritual path. Cherry said that the most I could bring was four. Many people can easier commit to the less frightening Dalai Lama than Hindu masters, plus staying at Cherry's is an easy sell. So, this time, I brought three others with me—my sister, Linda Young, and friends, Jeanie Knight and Vernon Arnold—a good number to travel with—good people and interesting conversations. We drove to Winslow, Indiana, to get Vernon, and then he drove to Bloomington.

We brought house gifts for Cherry. Everyone got along.

I tried to impress on everyone the importance of going early to get a good seat, but Vernon unexpectedly dropped us off on the way to the lecture, so he could visit a friend. He came back for us with just enough time to reach Assembly Hall (the basketball stadium).

So, finally, **August 18, 1999, we reached Assembly Hall.** I couldn't convince Linda, that because of security, her large purse might not be allowed in. The guards made us take her purse back to the car. Finally, we were allowed inside, but in the last row, high into the rafters. Jeanie and I sit together, and about twenty people to our right, Linda sits with Vernon. We can barely see, and hear very little ... but everyone is quiet and attentive ... a great energy. Jeanie and I hold hands. There is a powerful and pure healing energy between us, like we are thirteen again. It is a blessing just to be here.

There was a much longer, expensive Kalachakra Empowerment Initiation and consecration of a Kalachakra Stupa for World Peace and Harmony going on August 16–28, but we couldn't afford it.

September 7, 2003, the Dalai Lama came back to Bloomington— this time for the Dedication of the Chamtse Ling interfaith temple at 10:00 am and a Youth Program at 2 pm.

I came early to Cherry's on Saturday, September 6th. This time with old friend Carey Smith and two friends of his that I'd recently met, Julie Little and Penny Murphy.

We attended Cherry's Yoga Class at 12:30 pm. It was very good. She's very knowledgeable about the Hatha (physical) Yoga. At the end we did some of the Sufi walks, which developed calm, yet energizing feelings.

We had time to walk through the woods. I took Julie down the path to where the hippies live. There's a bell you ring when getting close. Julie calls the path Hippie Trail. Not many people there, but each time, it's different ones. This time there was a nice young mother with two of her own kids and one she was watching. They took us down to the stream to wade and collect fossils. I did magic tricks for the kids, and taught them the Sikh Children's Chant. The mother liked the chant, and had me write it down.

That night we all went to Indianapolis to see Cherry's teacher of thirty years, Swami Veda Bharati. Cherry's teacher is a gentle, knowledgeable man, who teaches through the Himalayan Institute of Swami Rama. We are in a small crowded room with attentive, respectful devotees. Even though tired from only having slept ten minutes the night before, the energy in the room makes me alert and calm. It seems I can never be prepared enough to absorb the refined energy and advanced teachings of these rare and blessed holy gatherings. It is said that if one is ready, one glance from an enlightened master is enough. I have had many such glances, and am continuously trying to be prepared.

Nice energy is building. The trip is already worth it, yet the event we came for doesn't start until tomorrow. This happens a lot. Some traditions consider the journey there and back, as a part of the gathering.

Sunday, September 7, 2003, I stretched, had a great breakfast, and headed for the Tibetan Cultural Center with the others. We parked across the street in a large parking lot. Our entry fee was seventy-five dollars each. The dedication ceremony was on a stage under a huge tent. We sat in our assigned seats. Other dignitaries and celebrities were there: Muhammad Ali, Chinese actress Bai Ling, and others. After the ceremony, the dignitaries went to the side of the temple to plant a peace tree. The Dalai Lama playfully grabbed a camera and took a photo of Muhammad Ali—everyone who saw it laughed.

During the break before the Youth Program, I went walking around—ran into Dennis Jackson, who I hadn't seen in years. He's now living in Alaska.

I was a little late coming to the afternoon session, and saw a crowd playfully running after someone. Upon closer scrutiny, I see that the man they are following is handing out something. I get into the herd, reach out my hand like the others, and receive some seeds or beads. The only information I could get at the time was from a Tibetan man who didn't speak much English. I got that the beads were blessed by the Dalai Lama. I have since tried to sprout some, with no luck. I've given some away, and have a few left.

The Youth Program starts. The theme is: "How to Find Peaceful Solutions to Conflicts." Local youth competed in an essay contest to win a place on the stage. Each youth is paired with a celebrity.

Muhammad Ali was partially introduced as the man who collects more money for charity than anyone now alive on the planet. This sent "uhs" ringing out throughout many in the audience. Ali's daughter Hana read a poem Ali had written (Ali has Parkinson's). She messed up part of it, and humbly, graciously, admitted her error, then read the poem flawlessly. Here is that poem:

If it is peace we wish to attain, then peace must start within. Before there can be peace in the world, there must be peace in our everyday lives. There should be peace in our actions, peace in our thoughts, peace in our voices when we speak, and peace in our hearts.

The Dalai Lama said that he had seen many of Muhammad Ali's matches on TV, but if he were to step in the ring with Ali, he would surely be knocked down with the very first punch.

Chinese film star Bai Ling spoke of the peacefulness she felt the closer she got to Bloomington. She is banned from China after co-starring with Tibetan Buddhist advocate Richard Gere in the movie *Red Corner*.

The Dalai Lama's highly respected sister, Jetsun Pema, was on the panel. She heads the Tibetan Children's Village in Dharamsala, India. She has recently been given the title "Mother of Tibet."

Elaine Mellencamp, super-model and wife of rock star John Mellencamp, was also on the panel.

The MC was Robert Thurman, a college professor for over thirty years, and holder of the first endowed chair in Buddhist Studies in the West, at Columbia University. He was the first Western Tibetan Monk, and a long time student and friend of the Dalai Lama. He is the father of actress Uma Thurman. He communicates extremely well and can be very funny.

Patrick O'Mara, dean of IU's Office of International Programs, gave Ali an IU sweatshirt. With a grin on his face, Ali replied, "Is this all I get?"—many laughed, including me.

The students spoke, and some read parts of what they'd written. They were all bright, articulate, and perceptive.

The next day we drove back to Evansville, stopping to eat at the Amish restaurant in Washington, Indiana.

The last time I saw the Dalai Lama was in 2007. He was in Bloomington October 23–28. Cherry had recently had some episodes of short-term memory loss. She did seem very coherent over the phone, but as a precaution I decided to only go with one other person. I went with Manna Wightman. Manna was raised as a Mormon. When young she was called goody-two-shoes because she actually lived the moral principles that the church espoused. I taught her some of the vigorous Sikh Yoga. She felt it quicker than anyone I've ever taught. We also did Rudi's Technique.

Before going to Bloomington we went to Chicago to participate in a gathering of a Jedi Realism group that Manna belongs to. They are very nice people, who are also open and disciplined—the kind of people who can progress very rapidly in Yoga. They are also into martial arts. I taught them some Yoga, and spoke with most of them individually.

Some of them did absorb unusually quick. One of the participants came all the way from England. The next year I was with the same organization in Lincoln State Park in Indiana. That time I did some Sikh Numerology (which is remarkably accurate), and taught them Rudi's Technique. Most of the ones there had also been in Chicago.

Now back to 2007. **October 23, 2007**, we left Chicago early for Bloomington. We had to pick up our tickets at IU Auditorium, and weren't sure how long it would take.

We easily got our tickets, and then went to eat with Cherry at Blooming Foods Restaurant inside their health food store. Later, I went with Cherry to her Yoga Class that she taught at Indiana University, and then back to Cherry's for the night.

Cherry played this incredibly beautiful CD by her son Matt's group *The Klezmatics*. *The Klezmatics* won the 2006 Grammy Award for the Best Contemporary World Music Album with this CD that they titled "*Wonder Wheel*." It puts some of the poetry of Woody Guthrie to music.

This time, the Dalai Lama is to give a teaching on *Atisha's Lamp for the Path to Enlightenment*. Manna and I paid for the full course at $275 each. There were three recommended books for the course. I read one and skimmed another. Atisha clearly, systematically, explains the path of Tibetan Buddhism. The teaching has already helped me, as I was dealing with a man who had stolen from me. I turned my hatred, which felt like I was poisoning myself, into compassion for this man, by feeling sorry for the conditions that had turned him into a greedy person, and tried to think of a way to help him.

The morning of October 24, 2007, we drove into the city for the first of six lectures—two a day for three days. We were to park in the Atwater Parking Garage, and then take the shuttle to IU Auditorium. We had to be there fifteen minutes early or lose our reserved seats. Parking was slower than hoped for, and then the garage attendant said that she didn't know anything about a shuttle.

We quickly walk through campus—around buildings and through lawns. Then we finally see the road that the auditorium is on. Walking up to an intersection, I see the Dalai Lama with a small entourage of Buddhist Monks. We reach the intersection at the same time. I calmly slow down, respectfully put my hands together, and bow to His Holiness. He does the same to me. I step in a few feet behind him and just to his right. The last few blocks to the auditorium, I am the closest to him. During this walk, the recurring pain in my back and knees is completely gone. I am light and strong.

Later, I found out that on October 17th, the Dalai Lama was presented the prestigious Congressional Gold Medal, the highest award to be bestowed on a civilian by the United States Government. And that the Chinese Government vehemently protested this award being given to him. There was strict security, even a Homeland Security Van, for the rest of the festivities—which makes it even more remarkable that I could have just casually walked up to the Dalai Lama.

In the auditorium, an oriental man plays a stringed instrument and sings, then some dancers.

Then the Dalai Lama speaks. Some of the things he says: My Christian friends consider me as a good Christian. ♦ I awake at 3:30 am. ♦ A Christian friend said, "This very life created by God." ♦ Don't make effort to propagate Buddhism, unless asked. ♦ Reverend Moon's people give Mongolians fifteen dollars to convert—same ones convert each year. ♦ Just smile when no good answer. ♦ All religions provide ground of hope. ♦ I have difficulty having compassion for mosquitoes. ♦ At six or seven I had no interest in learning. ♦ My knowledge is very limited, but when it comes to explaining that knowledge, I'm not that bad. ♦ Atisha was originally in Sanskrit. Sanskrit is a sacred language. ♦ I'm not a great scholar—just know hodgepodge. ♦ I had trouble memorizing when I was young. ♦ Because the mind is limited, we are polluted.

After a break, we came back for the second session at 2:00 pm. Beau Badeaux sat next to me. He's an IU student originally from the Bayou region. He had just gotten a book on the Dalai Lama, and then was surprised to hear the he's actually coming here. Beau keeps incredibly good notes—when I nod off (because of lack of sleep), I can usually peek at his notes to catch up. As the course progressed many people began taking notes because of the increasing depth and insightfulness of the course. Plus, the Dalai Lama may be the world's greatest expert on what he teaches. This is actually the first time I've really studied the

Tibetan Buddhist teachings. Previously it was the Dalai Lama's presence, opening others to the spiritual path, and visiting Cherry. Beau jokingly said that I cheated, because I'd read one of the books before coming—it sure made it a lot easier to understand.

I won't simply repeat the teachings here—they can be found elsewhere. I'll just mention some points that really struck me, or, are somewhat interesting. A lot of the basics overlap with other spiritual traditions that I've studied. I was particularly struck by some specifics His Holiness gave for overcoming our real enemies ... our mental afflictions. I will do further study on this, after this course.

At one point, when the Dalai Lama was explaining the true nature of the Self, his interpreter, who also seemed like a very wise person, simply gave a big sigh. Many laughed, including me, realizing the extreme difficulty of his task. Some other thoughts of His Holiness: Reality of the Self ... separate from senses and intellect ... must be eternal, unitary, and independent. ♦ Buddhists say the Self is the aggravate of its parts. Self can't be found in simple elements or outside them; then it is the combination. ♦ We do exist as a contingent notion. ♦ Objective observation leads to nothing. Even unconditional reality is empty. Seeing material things as real is the fundamental ignorance.

That night Cherry, Manna, and I went to IU Auditorium to hear Robert Thurman speak. He was very interesting and entertaining. We ran into Cherry's friend Shehira Davezac and her ex-student Phil. I first met Shehira here in 1996. Shehira was with Robert Thurman years ago when he injured an eye changing a tire on a motorcycle.

The new president and director of the center is Arjia Rinpoche and the center's name is now Tibetan Mongolian Buddhist Cultural Center. Arjia appears to be a wise, experienced, and humble man. The Dalai Lama has changed the temple's name to Kumbum Chamtse Ling in honor of the great Kumbum Monastery located in Eastern Tibet.

Thursday, October 25, 2007, had a wonderful breakfast of granola, whole milk, banana, tea, and peanuts with Manna and Cherry—then off with Manna for session number three. There is a pattern developing that I stay up late talking with Cherry, which I really want to do, but then I don't get much sleep. Yet, I still wake up early enough to do Yoga before breakfast. I never found the time to fully read the clippings of

Cherry's son Matt's music Grammy, which was hanging on the kitchen bulletin board.

I was hoping to see the Dalai Lama like I did yesterday. I got to the same spot, at the same time, but he wasn't there.

Going through security, I had forgotten I had a camera in my pocket, but they let me in with a promise not to use it.

Inside the auditorium, session three, the Dalai Lama bows to all. I bow back, and feel a physical energy with the bow. There is greater energy than yesterday. People are more attentive, quieter, and more respectful. There are more note takers and bigger notebooks. Here are some of my notes: Karma is illusion. ♦ The extreme of solitary peace is lacking in courage. ♦ Live morally to gain a good birth. ♦ Subtleties of Karma are beyond the intellect, so faith is necessary. Worldly concerns are secondary.

The fourth session is due to start at 2:00 pm. I spoke briefly with Missy Knight from Evansville. Waiting in my seat, I met one of the people in front of me, Sara Skelly. She's a very nice lady who lives just east of St. Louis. This trip is a gift from her husband. Her guru has passed. She has an older relative whose last name is Read, which means we could be related. Beau, who sits directly behind her, says he first met her when he fell asleep on the back of her chair.

Some of my notes from that session: Compassion is better than pity. ♦ Family compassion is not as good as universal compassion. ♦ Realistic fears are not as bad as unreal fears. ♦ Share other's pain. You gain strength and confidence because you do it voluntarily. ♦ Tomorrow we will do the *Aspirational Ritual*—it's very important. ♦ Balance the inhale and exhale. ♦ We can get *Calm Abiding* by focusing on our own minds. ♦ Imagine Buddha six feet in front of brow and bright, also heavy … this limits mental excitation. ♦ Think of death and impermanence if you are too excited. ♦ Short meditations are best, so you don't get weary, like throwing an extra log to keep the fire going. ♦ Some deity practices and breathing practices can also get *Calm Abiding*. Need emptiness as basis of deity meditation, or can reinforce clinging to existence.

Back to Cherry's for the night. She says that the old remedy for joint pain is Arnica. We spoke of much, including plans for the fire ceremony here tomorrow. She's done it several times before, when I've been here. Great energy—one of the things I really look forward to.

Friday morning, October 26, 2007, session number five starts with young monks chanting. Then going more rapidly through more of the sixty-eight verses of "*The Lamp for the Path to Enlightenment*"— we're now at verse forty-one.

Some specifics that I'm drawn to: Cure for hatred is to meditate on love. ♦ Cure for attachment is to meditate on the impurity of the body—though can do this too long. ♦ Cure for delusion is to become more grounded. Delusion is the basis of anger and other afflictions. ♦ The cure for illusion applies to all afflictions. The wisdom of emptiness is the cure.

We took the vow "*Generating the Mind for Enlightenment*." The Dalai Lama was invited to come back in 2009.

Session six is actually at Purdue University, but we see it here by live video. The title is "Cultivating Happiness."

Here are some quotes from that session: My broken English also getting old. ♦ Special power or miracle power—I don't have. Please don't expect much. Mentally, emotionally, physically, we are the same. ♦ The Queen of England told me that humanity is doing better. ♦ Generally people are more mature. CEOs helping fight diseases, like AIDS. ♦ With a broader view we are getting better. ♦ About Iraq War, I don't know. ♦ I enjoyed meeting President Bush—as a person, I love him. ♦ Women are more sensitive. My mother never showed me anger. ♦ We should take a strong stance against genocide, but with compassion.

That night, Cherry did the Fire Ceremony. John Hicks came. I helped some with the chanting, as it's a chant I know, *Mrutyunjaya*. I didn't know this chant the other times Cherry had done the ceremony.

Saturday, October 27, 2007, a nice leisurely morning. Only event scheduled is the Dalai Lama's talk at 2:00 pm at assembly Hall. Cherry and I gossip. Cherry showed me an interesting letter she has from Swami Chetanananda. She spoke of her unstable neighbor lady, who she once found outside hiding behind mailboxes, without a shirt on.

I spoke some with Beth Tobin, a nice woman who helps Cherry pay her bills.

We had to pack, because after Assembly Hall we're heading home.

Manna was hurrying me, so we'd get a good seat—the exact opposite
of the first day, when I was hurrying her.

At Assembly Hall, we're settled in extremely cramped seats. Next
to me is Katelyn Hudson, an IU student from Louisville. She's funny,
bright, and studying French. Next to Manna is a Japanese woman
named Marion, who lives in San Francisco. Elaine Mellencamp speaks,
then the Indiana University President.

Finally, it's the Dalai Lama's turn. He bows to the audience, then
waves his hand downward, while quickly saying, "Sit down."—people
laugh. Much of the talk was a repeat of other talks, but a few new or
interesting statements are: The past, whether good or bad, disappears
into space. ♦ I'm just another human being. In some extent, I think
I'm spoiled. ♦ Chairman Mao told me, "Religion is poison." The Dalai
Lama says that that was the last time he saw him—implying that there
was no possibility of further dialogue. ♦ If you forget, that is no ground
for forgiveness. ♦ If you think the real danger is one of losing your
compassion, then you are really living compassion. I was talking to a
friend who was imprisoned in China for years. I asked him if he was
ever afraid. He answered, "Yes, several times." I said, "What were you
afraid of?" He said, "I was afraid of losing my compassion."

The seat hurt my back and knees. I had to get up and walk around.
There were a lot of wonderful booths. I found a bookstall. Describing
to the saleswoman what I wanted, she pointed to the smallest book—
the only one I could afford.

We made it back to Evansville with only a few dollars left. Several
times, Manna said, "This is a blessed trip." I believe she was right.

Chapter Twelve: Stray Visions and Insights

This chapter is visions and insights that I feel like sharing, but that don't fit into one of the other chapters.

Sometimes, things would just come to me. Like once, walking late in a area I wasn't familiar with, I had a strong impulse to walk around a specific block. When on the other side, I looked back and saw several large men drinking while leaning on a car.

When the feeling/thought wasn't connected to anything logical, that was sometimes a sign that it was true.

Another time, while applying for a photography job (my only really marketable skill), I was focusing on my application while sitting in the waiting room. Looking down, I saw this well dressed, shapely woman walk by me. My curiosity got the best of me, as I looked up to see what she looked like, hoping she wouldn't be distractingly attractive. She had the chiseled features of an Aztec Goddess. I'm managing to not speak to her, when this absurd thought came to me, that she had the same name and birthday as my first wife. I foolishly walked up to her and asked if her name was Patti and her birthday April 18th. Her answer was, "Yes."

We were together for several months. Near the end, when the arguments were becoming more intense and frequent, there was a particularly powerful encounter. Feeling myself being pulled into a useless vortex, I closed my eyes and focused on the crown chakra. Very clearly, I heard hundreds of voices blissfully singing *"AUM"*. Patti became even more upset, and our relationship ended later that day.

One long, difficult, but fulfilling day, I worked in my garden in the fresh air and sunshine. Walking to the house, I stopped to rest against the metal, swing frame. At that moment, I ceased to be limited, infinite energy came into me, and infinite energy left me.

I became aware that if I felt a person or circumstance to be either strongly negative or positive, it often was. This led me away from bad circumstances and towards good ones.

One night, I went to sleep meditating on the darkest area in my room, seeing it calmer and more substantial than light. Upon waking in the morning, for a few seconds, I saw the stars within my head.

Once I had a date with an attractive, educated, and well traveled woman. The date was pleasant, but I kept putting off calling her, although not knowing why. Months passed, and then I ran into her mother. The young woman had died. She was riding with a man who wrecked his car on purpose, killing both of them. Sometimes since, I can tell if someone is going to die soon. It's like their spirit is already starting to leave.

I got a message from all three of the people who raised me … after they passed. When my grandmother died I was living in Michigan and couldn't get home for the funeral. I looked for an open church on this freezing Wednesday in the middle of winter. I found one open and walked in, but no one was there. Sitting in a pew, I close my eyes and pray. Lines of pleasing energy, the size of my little finger, begin traveling through my brain for several minutes. I take this as a sign that grandma is OK.

When mother passed, I was at her funeral, and even read her favorite poem. It was 1994. She had been initiated into Transcendental Meditation in 1972. She had told me her secret mantra shortly after getting it, but I hadn't thought of it in many years, assuming that I had completely forgotten it. But at her funeral, her mantra repeated clearly and rhythmically in my mind for several minutes.

The other person that raised me was my uncle A L. Years after he had passed; I awoke one morning with a plain black and white dream going through my mind. In the dream, I walk into the kitchen, and lean against a small counter next to a wall. To my right someone walks into the room and places a box on top of the large, kitchen table. The box flipped open like a pizza box. The man walked to the kitchen sink, turned, and leaned against the sink. At this point, the dream is now in color. I clearly see that the man is my uncle. I can count every hair on his head. He's younger and thinner than I remembered him. He looks to be in his twenties. His full black hair is neatly combed back. He's clean shaved and tan. He wears an attractive, colorful shirt, tucked in neatly in creased, dark pants.

I tried to focus so I would remember details, yet be calm so the vision would stay. After a very long fifteen seconds, the vision faded away.

I knew I had to tell each of my five siblings, but expected skepticism from them, because none of them are into metaphysics. I told each one-on-one, and each surprised me by being open and respectful.

My daily meditations would often bring insights, but when I taught a Yoga class it would be even more intense. I would prepare for at least several hours for each class, then surrender at the class, and sometimes say something that I didn't know until I heard myself say it.

This very nice, young couple came to a few classes. They tried to talk me into allowing their five-year, old daughter to come. I finally relented, saying that I would give the child pillows and toys. She would be free to attend any portion of the class she wanted.

In the class the child attended, she walked over to the rest of us when we were doing a Sikh chant ... she then led the chant, doing it in a Punjabi accent. These were Americans who had never seen a Sikh. The girl had also drawn pictures of people in turbans before she had ever heard of a turban.

I met the family's youngest child when he was in the back seat of the family car. I open the back door, stick my head in ... and am in another dimension. It felt like I was in the presence of a saint ... I couldn't speak.

One of the places I taught was far from my home, and the class ended after the buses stopped running, so I would often spend the night at the Yoga Center. I would listen to tapes and read much of the material at the center.

I read Reiki books. The founder of Reiki spent two weeks in an Eastern monastery, then taught what he said was the ultimate knowledge. Curious, I attended several of the Reiki open sessions—but felt nothing. Then once, my Yoga class ended early and I was putting on my shoes. Behind the door, close to me, an advanced Reiki initiate's class was going on. The leader was clear and articulate. I stayed for some twenty minutes, listening to see were this talk would go. Then it ended. It didn't go anywhere. You could pick up more insight from the average person you'd meet at a neighborhood bar.

After years of meditating, I found out that I could read the Bible and now get something out of it. I had been questioning for months why I hadn't had a vision of Jesus, when I had visions of other saints.

Then one day, a dream came, starting ordinary, a black and white ballroom, with small groups of people talking, like after a concert—canvassing the small scattered groups, I see one man standing alone … he's looking directly at me … instantly, I know it's Jesus. He's short and stocky; with a full-body robe that also covers has head. He has a square jaw with a short black beard. Most impressive is his deep, dark eyes. I look into his eyes, as he is looking at me. I surrender and penetrate deep into his eyes … continuously surrendering … continuously going deeper. Then it ends.

At a Pentecostal Church in Evansville, I had a brief vision of Lord Dattatreya.

When living in Michigan, I decided to go to every church. Having gone to mainly a Methodist, I wanted to see what the others were really like. My favorite became Unity. Once, I was even a guest speaker there. My next favorite was Seven Day Adventist. These two spent much less time criticizing others, and thus, much more time in actual study and devotion. The sermons at a Primitive Baptist were by far the most re-searched and uplifting. My least favorite was the Unitarian Church, which didn't even seem like a church as it openly accepted immoral behavior. In between were all the other churches, with the Pentecostal Churches having the strongest healing energy, yet the most egotistical sermons. The Mormon Church had the least metaphysical knowledge, but because of strong health and morality principles they make a good social organization.

I met people from an organization that ran psychic fairs. I audi-tioned, and was set to work at their next fair. I was told I could do one a week but wouldn't make a profit until I'd worked several.

At this first one, I did make a profit, as people were coming back to me and bringing their friends. I did the Sikh Numerology (which is very accurate), the holding hand thing I did when with Maharishi, and this unusual Tarot deck. To pay homage to the Sikhs that taught me the Sikh Numerology, I wore a turban when doing readings. I would also give the clients meditations that suited them.

There's an expectation and openness at these fairs that most people don't usually have, thus they get high. People will come back for this high even when they were given inaccurate information at previous fairs. There's a lot of self-deception and some outright deception. Only two of the other readers seemed to have psychic abilities, but neither of them could use it constructively.

A few hours into the fair, the leader came up to me and said that I couldn't work the next few fairs because of seniority. Later, she told me that I couldn't work some others because they were full. So, I was being hustled, also.

Another reader, a nice older lady, would sometimes speak of her connection to celebrities and heads of state. Some of the other readers didn't believe her, but I liked her energy, so became friends with her. Several weeks later, I visited her at her home, and saw photos of her with the people she had mentioned.

A few months later, I was working a psychic fair in Bloomington, Indiana. Several of the other readers brought a woman to me, and then told her, "He will help you." Most of the readings are fluff, but after a few minutes, I realized that this woman could easily leave this building and kill herself. I then realized that our respective roles were interfering with any real communication, so had to drop my role as a reader.

We're talking, I understand her more, but it's not enough. I keep surrendering, searching for an answer. Then it comes to me—she is like someone from my distant past. Both her, and the woman from my past, are people of extraordinary gifts and potential, but when they connect to ordinary people, ordinary people are incapable of fulfilling them. I then help her to see her situation more clearly, by honestly analyzing, and looking from a broader perspective. She left in a better and clearer mood.

I would sometimes go to this Hari Krishna house for the good meals and chanting. One day I went there, and all but one of the devotees were at a conference. The remaining devotee partially dropped his guard, as we knew some of the same people. He's telling me stories of Krishna, most of which I'd already heard. There's a huge poster of Krishna dancing with the milk maids, on the wall next to me. Looking at that poster, I imagine that its scene is real, and my ordinary life is but a dream. The room disappears, all is darkness … only remaining is my consciousness … what I've directly experienced … all else is but a dream.

In a dream, I was sitting on the floor with other students. A bearded teacher was in front of us holding a copper sheet with a Sri Yantra engraving. The teacher walked past me, and I followed. We went into a deep forest to a small area where sunlight filtered through. The teacher said, "Meditate on the particles within the light."

A few days ago, in April of 2009, while riding the city bus, for a few seconds I could clearly see the chakras within the other passengers … multi-colored, blissful, wheels of light—spinning in perfection.

One last vision was as real and blissful as any Darshan I've had with a living saint. An old, thin holy man is sitting on a stone wall that runs beside a dirt road. He has one foot on the road and the other foot on the thigh of the first leg … I am in ecstasy … a strong blissful consciousness creates a desire to never leave. Looking back on this vision, my best guess is that it was Ramana Maharshi.

Chapter Thirteen: Babaji, the Ageless Master

I first heard of Babaji at the rock festival in Louisiana in 1971, as mentioned at the end of chapter three. There I was taught the chant: *Om Kriya Babaji Namah Om.*

Later that summer, coming home from Maharishi's retreat in California, I first read of Babaji in *Autobiography of a Yogi.*

In December, 1986, I traveled to Washington, D.C., to be initiated into the linage of Babaji by a direct disciple of his, Yogi Ramaiah.

During the ride to D.C., the Babaji chant from Louisiana came through me spontaneously. I hadn't thought of it in many years, and was surprised that I remembered it. It seemed to be in perfect pitch and rhythm … magically lifting me into timeless wonders, where celestial music is our basic nature and fifteen years is just a few minutes ago.

Before the initiation, there was a religious conference with speakers from various paths.

Then we went to the Maryland suburb where the actual initiation was to take place. It was an ordinary looking home, but with a small ornate temple in the back yard.

My traveling companion, Dennis Jackson, and I arrived a little early. We were sent to a small upstairs room where some of the male initiates slept on the floor in sleeping bags.

There we met a wandering *sannyasin* (one who has taken spiritual vows) who was given his robes by Master Subramuniya. The sannyasin, Baba Nataraja, entertained us for several hours with stories of his life, information about Babaji, and healing secrets.

The night before the initiation was to officially start, there were about twenty of us sitting in the main room. Yogi Ramaiah (Yogiar) was interpreting some Tamil scriptures into English. I listened intently, and tried to *feel* what he was saying. The scriptures were describing, among other things, the movement of consciousness up the chakras. As I moved upward through the chakras, by Yogiar's guidance, I would feel various emotional states, and *then* Yogiar would describe the emotion I was feeling. Yogiar would become angry at those transcribing if they moved too slowly. There were definite lengths of time to spend in each chakra, and by moving too slowly some of the accumulating energy is lost.

It was a great blessing to be there. I had already gained more than expected, yet the course had not officially begun.

The week long initiation was like boot camp—difficult physical Yoga with only a few hours to sleep. We had to memorize Tamil words and weren't allowed to take notes. I developed a headache, sore throat, chills, and drained energy.

One of my fellow initiates, Chris Johnson, had spent years going through the full range of instructions of the Self Realization Fellowship, the organization left by Paramahansa Yogananda. Chris said the week here surpassed everything that he'd learned at SRF.

Several blocks away was a fine health food restaurant that I'd been to years earlier. Once, while walking there, my breath was deep and powerful, filling the whole body with energy … I could feel the joyous strength and spring of individual muscles.

December 22, the final stage of the initiation, I'm sitting with the others … eyes closed in meditation. Clearly, I see Annai (Babaji's consort) as she appears in a photo that's in the room.

I smell green grass, cool fresh air, and the otherworldly blissful aroma of extreme health. *Om Kriya Babaji Namah Om* … Babaji is chanting it, or comes in with it, or is it. He enters from my left side. I eat one of his favorite fruits, it's tasty; but more than that, brings energy to my subtle body. I feel the ground. I feel the hands of Babaji and Annai (as she comes out of meditation). Babaji's hand is warm and strong … giving me energy. Annai's hand receives my energy … she is fluid, cool, and blissful. Sri Ganapati Sachchidananda Swamiji (chapter 14) joins us. Swamiji enters from my left. My mind tries to manipulate, is confused as to what is real, settles back and surrenders to a deeper dimension. I am emotionally happy, blissful, and my human insecurities and clinging are pushed aside by the scene. Now, Babaji is sitting in front of me, Annai to my right, and Swamiji to my left. Babaji's outline remains, but the inner details dissolve … briefly, I see and feel the chakras spinning inside Babaji … the chakras fade and the stars and planets emerge, stretching to infinity. I feel the tremendous energy and awareness with which Babaji can simultaneously guide thousands. I turn facing Swamiji … the same is within Swamiji. With my eyes closed, as Yogiar starts speaking again, I feel Babaji's energy in the room, flowing through Yogiar, and Babaji's photo. Coming out of the meditation, I see a photo of Annai on the opposite wall … blissful waves float from Annai to me.

Just remembering this experience gives me a blessing … the stars and planets within Babaji and Swamiji … the vastness which is our nature.

I've had marvelous meditations practicing the techniques of Babaji in the preceding years … feeling the subtle effects of mantras, relaxation, energy, and sometimes experiencing my past in greater detail than when it was experienced the first time … going to a wider circle of experience, from where the old small *me* is just a self-caged illusion.

It is said that just by saying Babaji's name with reverence one receives a blessing. I've experienced this many times myself.

Chapter Fourteen: Ganapati Sachchidananda, Swamiji

In 1985 there was a poster in the Health Food Co-op in Evansville about Sri Ganapati Sachchidananda Swamiji. Swamiji was coming nearby to Evansville's satellite city of Newburgh, Indiana. I had heard very little of Swamiji, so had few expectations; particularly, since it was just a little town in Indiana.

I walked up to the average-looking suburban home, put my shoes beside the others, and knocked on the door. I humbly stated that I'd like to see the Swami—thinking my ego would just safely blend into the background.

I was ushered in. A small group of Indians were standing just inside the door. To the left was a small open room with Swamiji sitting on a couch against the far wall. Swamiji was a powerful looking man with a long black beard and the traditional orange robe of the renunciate.

I was told, "You can see Swamiji now." Surprised, but with respect, I walk to kneel before Swamiji with my hands in prayer pose. A few words are exchanged. I'm surrendering to the higher Self. Swamiji's hands briefly embrace mine. Swamiji's eyes close. I close my eyes and surrender … warm, blissful waves travel up and down inside my spine. For several weeks, I had more energy on all levels, and it was automatically directed in the best possible direction. During that period, I was incapable of negative thought.

I was told that Swamiji rarely touches people.

Beside the Indian sponsors, Missy and Danny Knight were also there.

In 1986 Swamiji returned. This time the pace was more hectic, with more activities and more people—still with very few Americans.

Once, I went to the same house as in 1985 to attend a music concert. The home was very crowded. Swamiji entered, and everyone rose. We moved to the sides to allow Swamiji and the musicians to get to the stage. Walking past me, Swamiji turns and says, "How are you?" I say something polite … the feeling is, that I'm reuniting with my dearest friend, of a depth of friendship far greater than any I've ever experienced.

One evening, I asked Swamiji if we could meditate together like last year. Swamiji told me to come see Swamiji (I've heard that to use a pronoun instead of *Swamiji* is considered inappropriate) at a set time the next morning.

I was several minutes late, but Sri Swamiji (*Sri* is a term of respect or endearment) was very busy, anyway. There were people rushing in and out of Swamiji's room, making plans and seeking advice.

I was sure that this wouldn't interfere with Swamiji's promise to meditate with me. I found a long, empty, out-of-the-way, wooden bench. I sat, closed my eyes, relaxed, and continuously let go of whatever appeared.

My awareness drifts down; close to the navel ... all is darkness, calm. From the navel, I'm looking in towards the spine. Where the spine was, there's a spinning wheel. The thought comes, "I must be imagining it." I let the wheel go, but it stays, even coming in clearer. The wheel is spinning by its own power ... a blissful feeling of pure, effortless, constant energy. A ring of flower petals point downward from its circumference. The petals are of various luminous colors; and more vivid, by far, than any colors I've seen in the material dimension. On top of the wheel is a silver Being, sitting on a silver throne. I'm transformed to a feeling of freedom, joy, and boundless wonder. I become vaguely aware of the outer, material dimension ... its vaporous, without any *real* substance, a dream. The vision fades. I'm back to ordinary consciousness; but I can never be the same, for now I know, from experience, a greater reality.

Just remembering this vision inspires me and brings great peace.

I was helping raise my great-niece, Crystal. I felt the need of a blessing for her, but failed in my attempt to secure an audience for her with Swamiji.

Just before Swamiji was to leave, on August 26, 1986, I was staying with my sister, Linda, several miles from Swamiji. The thought came to me, to take a photo of Crystal to Swamiji to be blessed.

The walk was longer and hotter than I expected. Walking up the drive, it looked as though they'd left. I was deciding what to do, when a van with Swamiji and Swamiji's entourage arrived.

Swamiji is closest to me, sitting in the front passenger seat. The others exit the other side and begin walking towards the house. Swamiji slowly comes out and takes a few steps in my direction. I'm gently pulled to Swamiji … nervousness and indecision dissolve.

I respectfully hand the photo to Swamiji, saying, "This is my greatniece Crystal, who I feel is a good soul, but needs your blessing to continue."

Swamiji takes the photo and looks into it. Swamiji's focusing creates expanded awareness in me. I'm alive to the pervasive, transcendental energy of the moment. The depth feels like forever … nothing else is needed.

Swamiji returns the photo, saying, "All right." With the clear understanding that the blessing is given.

Swamiji then walks to the house, and I leave.

Missy and Danny Knight again came to see Swamiji, as did Dennis and Beth Jackson, and my sister, Linda.

On December 22 of that year, I had a vision of Swamiji with Babaji, as told in chapter thirteen.

Swamiji returned to the United States in 1988.

This time I had the great privilege to go to Baton Rouge, Louisiana, to be initiated into Kriya Yoga by Swamiji. Kriya Yoga is a form of yoga mentioned in the Yoga Sutras of Sage Patanjali. This yoga deals with the activating and controlling of the five senses. When one controls the sense organs, there is a total control of the functioning of the thought process, which results in higher evolution of oneself. The Kriya initiation was July 26–28.

I stayed in a house with the musicians and Mukunda, a man from Trinidad. Besides the Kriya, there were concerts, *Pada Puja's* (wonderful rituals performed in followers' homes), meals, and discourses.

Each morning Swamiji performed *Sri Chakra Puja*, a purification ritual connected to the highest meditation. After one Sri Chakra Puja, Swamiji sat in a lounge chair, as about forty of us sat on the floor at Swamiji's feet. I was sitting about three feet to Swamiji's right. To Swamiji's left was a lady, for whom the night before, Swamiji had materialized a talisman with an engraving of Lord Datta on one side and Ganesh on the other.

The lady shows Swamiji a large crystal along with the talisman and a small rare crystal that grows in water. Swamiji asks for some water, and then asks for fire from the puja. Swamiji begins chanting, as Swamiji drips the water onto the hand that holds the talisman, and then moves the fire slowly back and forth underneath the talisman hand. Swamiji opens the talisman hand … now, there are two. Swamiji hands one to the lady saying, "I believe this one is yours … "—at this point, I surrender deeper, and am grateful just for being here—Swamiji turns to me, hands me the other talisman, and says—" … and this one is for you."

The side of the talisman with Lord Datta is facing me. Swamiji begins explaining to me who Lord Datta is … I'm surrendering deeper … the engraving of Lord Datta is brightly multi-colored, three-dimensional, and Lord Datta's arms are moving in a very graceful, mesmerizing dance. Swamiji stops speaking in mid-sentence and the talisman then appears to be a normal coin.

The talisman gave insight and healing. It would change temperature. Perceptive people would know exactly how long to hold it. After two years I lost it … or maybe, it just went away.

I spent a lot of time at the home of the local sponsors, Narendra and Nalini Dave. Nalini once told me that I seemed more Indian than American. They had two sweet little girls, Seema and Hina. I let the girls draw in my Kriya notebook and did magic tricks for them.

Once, some good classical music was playing on the radio. Hina began dancing. She was moving in graceful precision spins in perfect time to the music.

The next month, on August 2, 1988, Swamiji returned to Newburgh.

One evening, at the same home as in 1985 and 1986, we're settling in, in preparation for the music and discourse. One of the musicians brings me a tambourine and asks me to sit in with them. I politely take the tambourine and find a seat among the musicians, thinking that this is too good to be happening—that I'll just move quietly so they won't discover their mistake. I play background rhythm; or rather, it is played through me. Swamiji chants, talks, and plays the synthesizer. The music is of incredible artistic precision. It heals, brings awareness and incredible insights.

On August 4th there was a concert at St. Johns United Church of Christ in Evansville. The music, as always, was uplifting and healing. It's really beyond my ability to describe it—it has to be experienced, but even then it's beyond intellectual comprehension. My sister, Janet, and family friend, Beverly Nance, accompanied me to the concert.

Shortly after the concert ended, an Indian lady brought Swamiji a tray of flowers. Swamiji takes the flowers in Sri Swamiji's hands, and ashes fall between Swamiji's hands onto the tray. Sri Swamiji's hands then open … and the flowers are gone. The holy ash is distributed among the congregation. Janet is mumbling to herself in disbelief as we leave.

Many more people came for Swamiji's Darshan (holy presence) that year. Besides the ones already mentioned, among others, Missy and Danny Knight, Dennis and Beth Jackson, and Sue Shaffer came.

Swamiji returned to the United States in 1990.

I became aware of a pattern. Several months before Swamiji would arrive, I would be very poor and usually had some major health problem; but somehow, the money, strength, and free time necessary to see Swamiji, would come my way. I would also run into people who had seen Swamiji previously.

Again, I was blessed to be able to go to Baton Rouge. This time I was able to fly in, as opposed to taking a bus in 1988.

I arranged my flight to arrive on April 12, 1990, several hours before Swamiji and at the same airport. Upon arrival, I walked towards the gate that Sri Swamiji was scheduled to walk through. In front of me are about sixty Indians, waiting for Swamiji. A few of whom, I'd met in 1988. A few of the others have familiar faces. Even the ones I had seen, but never spoken to, felt like long lost friends … like we have an unbreakable spiritual connection. It seemed the only importance of the last two years, was to live morally enough to be worthy of Sri Swamiji's Darshan.

This time I stayed with a nice Indian couple, Dinesh and Sajel Sthanki, and three people originally from Trinidad, now living in New

York. I also was blessed to be the only non-Indian in Sri Swamiji's entourage.

I attended the Pada Pujas, chanted along with the others, and was sometimes given small chores.

One chore was to be the first person to the door of a new Pada Puja home. I would then inform the residents Swamiji has arrived, and hold the door open for Swamiji and entourage to enter.

Leaving one home, I feel a sudden upsurge of faith ... at that exact moment, Swamiji turns and smiles at me.

One particularly unostentatious home sticks out. This one is very crowded. After the rituals are performed, Swamiji sits at the family organ. Swamiji plays and chants ... the home is so thick with faith that I can feel the pervasive inner tears of joy. As Swamiji sings songs of heartfelt praise, a young boy works silently on a computer.

When the music has stopped, the boy brings Swamiji a printout of a large rose with words of praise to Lord Datta. I'm leaning in the doorway, just a few feet away. Swamiji touches the boy's cheek and pulls out a flower, then opens the flower and pulls out a small engraved talisman ... spontaneous sighs of wonder arise and joyous tears flow.

Another seva I was allowed to perform was as the cashier for the photos, books, and other items that were for sale.

Again, I got to spend time with little Seema and Hina. Once, the three of us were sitting in a van waiting for Swamiji and Swamiji's entourage. We were playing a riddle game. I felt something, looked up, and saw Swamiji smiling at us through a window.

Sometimes I would take the girls on short walks, and we'd chant the Sikh walking chant: *Ek Ong Kar-a, Sat-i Nam-a, Siri Wha-a, He Guru*. Once, I was hurriedly writing down the chant for Hina, as we prepared to leave for a short walk. Seema also wanted a copy. I told her we didn't have time. She began to cry. Her tears penetrated so deeply, that it was physically impossible to move before granting her wish. It wasn't so much that she was affecting me, but that deep inside we were the same.

Once, Hina asked me if I had any kids. The memory of my ex-step-daughter, Ajna, came clearly to my mind. I had to turn away from Hina to stop from crying. It had been ten years since I'd seen Ajna. I thought she was out of my mind. Hina's purity had opened my subconscious.

One evening there was a music and discourse session at Dinesh's brother Daulat's home. Before the concert, Swamiji was speaking quietly with some of the organizers. They were discussing the difficulty many Americans have with chanting. Swamiji looks at me and says, "With some it's no problem."

On this night, there was a short ceremony for a temple consecration. After the ceremony, Swamiji handed out some pieces of cotton that were for back problems. I was given one of the first pieces.

Before one of the concerts, my back is in so much pain that it doesn't seem as though I will even be able to sit. Determined to transcend the body, I imagine the silver cord, subtler that the body, extending through and beyond the spine. On the inhale, I breathe down the silver cord, and up on the exhale. During my better moments: Swamiji's music is playing the silver cord, I am energized and healed, and the body pain can't touch me.

One night I was taking a shower, slipped on the bathtub tile, and very forcefully hit my head on the side of the bathtub. I strongly objected to any pain or injury limiting my path, so immediately started thinking, "Jai Guru Datta." I wouldn't allow any negativity to enter.

The next morning I looked … there were no bruises and no pain.

Friday, April 20, 1990, I rode with Narayane Gonuguntla from Evansville to St. Louis to be with Swamiji.

Saturday, April 21, 1990, there was a Foundation Stone Laying Ceremony for the Hindu Temple of St. Louis. I had heard that the organizers were worried, because it had rained for several days and more rain was in the forecast. Swamiji was told of this concern. Swamiji then waved Sri Swamiji's hand towards the clouds … it didn't rain again until after the outdoor consecration.

The temple sight was very muddy. As part of the ritual, I walked barefooted through the mud, with a tray of bricks on my head. It reminded me of some of the better moments of the 1960's … freedom … joy … peace … love … brotherhood.

Around this time, I was talking to one of the Indian devotees. He said, "The reason I don't like you is because you are poor, and that means you are irresponsible." He apparently assumed that I already knew that he didn't like me, but this was my first indication.

Previously, I had done a sociological experiment. I had told a man who was adopted to only mention has father's prestigious position, and that the family gave him a house, car, and money to live on. The result of the experiment was that he was invited back and I wasn't. I later thought that my experiment was a mistake, when I found out that his mother and sister had a restraining order against him, and he was a drug dealer, among other things. I mentioned this to someone higher up in Swamiji's organization, but the response was that I had something personal against him, so, I just dropped it.

Maybe I should have mentioned that I am related to two ex-presidents, a signer of the Declaration of Independence, and an engineer on the Apollo Missions—all of which is true. Caste divisions aren't valid in our fluid society.

Speaking of caste, Swamiji has said: Always harping about greatness about Brahmins. This is sheer stupidity ... Who is a Brahmin?—anyone who does not eat meat or drink alcohol. Who observes discipline in life is a Brahmin ... Valmiki, Rama, Krishna were not Brahmins by birth ... Sri Rama, the hero of the great epic, was a Kshatriya ... You have to become Brahmin by your virtues, not by birth. I declare it today and I declare it forever. At the end of day, all that matters is if you are a good person, if you helped others, and if you lead a fulfilling life ... Your caste and creed should be limited to your Puja room in your house only. Once you come out of that room, you are a human. That is all ... I hate the idea of caste system.

Three years later, February 25, 1993, Swamiji returned to the United States.

On May 4, 1993, Swamiji arrived in Newburgh.

On May 5, 1993, I instinctively awoke very early and very refreshed. I began my spiritual practices, including *Lakshmi Stute*, a long chant to some of the feminine manifestations of God.

One of the verses is to *Dhairyalakshmidevi,* whose modest devotees are free from envy, anger, and fear, and whose intellect is free from distinctions.

While chanting this verse, I clearly see, for several seconds, a small village that is protected by this Goddess. I feel the villagers' freedom from envy, anger, and fear. Intuitively, I know that they are without distinctions and that by seeing the divine in all they don't allow negative qualities to enter. This also affects anyone that comes under their influence.

Once, I was blessed to feel, for a couple of seconds, the feminine aspects of the chakras. Another time, I was meditating on a photo of Lord Datta, asking for understanding of the difference between male and female. The photo became three-dimensional and solid. I then remembered Swami Nityananda explaining that male is subtle, female is concentrated, and both are of the same essence.

We must respect the opposite sex. Therein lies our wholeness … ego doesn't fit there.

I attend the morning Sri Chakra Puja. It's nice to see friends in the congregation, particularly, some who have yet to have Swamiji's Darshan.

As Swamiji's leaving, Swamiji stops and asks me, "How are you?"

I reply, "I've a problem with my back."—as I motion up and down my back with the right hand.

Later that day, I'm talking to a very amiable, perceptive professor from India. He points out to me that although I'm materially poor; I have the blessing of worship. This makes me realize my foolish character flaw of focusing on limitations instead of nourishing my incredible blessings. Blessings nourished grow to such vastness that problems become insignificant.

That night, at the apartment complex where the music and discourse were to shortly begin, I'm talking to two Indian ladies from Atlanta. One of them tells me she was born in Africa. I tell her that reminds me of the movie, *Mississippi Masala,* where the female lead's character was also an Indian who lived in Africa and then the Southern United States. She then informs me she has friends who know the actress that played the role. This sends a chill through my spine as I remember when I'd seen the movie, feeling I had a real life connection to that actress.

The concert room is stuffed with people, mostly Indians. I sit very close to the stage. This is the most blissful concert I've attended, before and after. I can somehow chant flawlessly with chants I've never heard before. Vibrations are more real than matter. My third eye is vibrating with the music. My soul is soaring. Tears of joy flow silently inside; as I return to a home my surface mind has forgotten. Swamiji speaks of our shared destiny, of our humanity, and of our blessings.

That night I only slept for an hour and a half, but was fully refreshed for the new day.

May 6, 1993, I attended the morning Sri Chakra Puja. As usual, Sri Swamiji gave me, as well as all others so inclined, a talisman after the puja. This talisman takes away some of our personal karmas.

A little later, Swamiji gave out food that was for healing chronic illness. I was given it first. Often remembering these moments with Swamiji, I'm actually aware of details I missed the first time. Time is relative.

That night the concert was at the Evansville Coliseum. I went with Linda, two neighbor kids, Leyna and Timmy Estes, and one kid I'd just met. The new kid's name was Brian Ethridge. Brian was listening to us discuss where we were going, and politely, yet strongly, asked to go. We drove several blocks, met his mother, and then went to the concert. Brian has a natural sense of right and wrong. I've seen him tell other children how to behave—and they listen to him.

May 7, 1993, I attended another Sri Chakra Puja. Shortly after the puja, we moved outside. Swamiji blessed a garland of roses, saying that these were for chronic illness. Swamiji gave the garland to Kali Ray, an American Yogi. She then distributed the roses. I received one.

In 1995 Swamiji returned. I didn't have the money that year. I tried to borrow but failed. I talked to everyone I knew, who might possible go, with no luck. Time running out, I'm dejectedly sitting at home when there's a knock on the door. It's Jackie Freeman. She says she wants to see Swamiji and will drive and pay all the expenses. Swamiji once said that he helps his devotees by putting thoughts in other people's minds—this could be an example of that.

It's now Monday, July 10, 1995. I'm at the Nicholson Post 38 of the American Legion in Baton Rouge, waiting for Swamiji. Its 9:05 am, Sri Chakra is scheduled for 9:30 am.

About three weeks ago, I was in my kitchen in Evansville. I felt pulled to the new Swamiji altar. The altar's in a doorless cabinet space that for several years, has been drawing me to consecrate an altar there. I relax and feel strong soothing energy, close my eyes, and clearly *see* Swamiji inside me, as clearly as if he is standing in front of me.

I hear Swamiji's thoughts, telling me to do one of the Kriyas that I rarely practice. I look up the Kriya and sit to begin. Instantly, I'm aware that I have a frighteningly intense headache and fever that are rapidly gaining power. After the Kriya, my headache and fever are completely gone. I then read that part of the affect of this Kriya is to reduce extreme heat. Since that day, I have more clearly, and consistently, felt Sri Swamiji's presence and guidance.

Back in Baton Rouge, Sri Chakra Puja is over. I bring a meditation shawl, I have just purchased, to Swamiji to be blessed. Swamiji says, through an interpreter, that I should wear it. I put the shawl around my shoulders, and then Sri Swamiji touches the shawl in blessing.

I saw old friends and made a few new ones.

This time, attending with Jackie and her sister, who are both new to this environment, I'm just one of the congregation, not helping with the work or part of Swamiji's entourage. It's not as exciting this way, but I'm sure I'm getting what I need. Swamiji has said, "God knows what we need." All we can do is be open and aware, and allow the actions that the awareness dictates.

I'm already feeling more centered and connected to my inner purity.

Waiting for Swamiji to arrive for the night music and discourse, I sit and do the Kriya for meditation on the chakras. Coming out of my meditation, I'm aware of the musicians playing and the congregation joyfully dancing. The music pulls me in. After several minutes, my knees begin to hurt. I choose to ignore the pain, and continue dancing. The dance continues for about half an hour. The pain doesn't increase and most of the time is less or even completely gone. This is the most I've been able to dance for several years.

Swamiji enters. Healing music follows, with wonderful stories of the saints, and instructions on how to tread the spiritual path.

Swamiji blesses some objects for me: two blue T-shirts with Swamiji's photo and the words "Guru Purnima, Baton Rouge, Louisiana, 1995";

the cassette *Celestial Message*, and a small bottle of holy water from Lake Manas Sarovar in the Himalayas.

Day one with Swamiji ends in deep, peaceful sleep. I wake early and refreshed, hours before the wake-up call.

July 11, 1995, during the morning Sri Chakra Puja the mantra *Hreem* repeats peacefully in my mind.

Swamiji says we are going to Brahma Loka, the world of Brahma, the Creator.

As is the custom, we've cleared a path for Swamiji to leave, with most people lined up on either side, in anticipation of Sri Swamiji's Darshan. Sometimes we're singing this wonderful chant for world peace: *Om Aim Hreem Shreem Shiva Rama Anagha Dattaya Namaha.* Sometimes there's a robust silence. I'm standing in one line, facing the other. Behind the line I'm facing, appears a holy man. A clear penetrating thought comes from him to me, "Why do you worry?"—with the definite meaning, that there is no need to worry, because I am on the perfect path. Then he disappears. So quickly does he leave, that it's difficult to grasp any definite features. There was a feeling that he was from the future, maybe my future. He seemed old (eighty-ish), powerful, a being of energy not flesh. He held a staff and wore very colorful, long garments with a hood, and a meditation shawl. His hair was long, dark and maybe braided. The message was more important than the appearance.

Later in the day, after Kriya Initiation, I'm just sitting. I retake the initiation every chance I get, because I always learn something new; and any excuse for being in Swamiji's presence brings a blessing. My back pain is much worse, extending the full length, and so intense I'm becoming frightened. Jackie asks if I'd like her to massage by back. I reply, "Yes." She comes over and gently massages my spine from the shoulder area slowly downward. Healing warmth from her hands takes away all the pain they touch. She's about three-fourths the way down. I'm feeling very contented. She says something like, "What did you do wrong to cause this pain?" Instantly, with this statement, her hands turn ice cold. Her hands no longer heal and are actually unpleasant. We talk about this, and she stops the massage.

The evening music has begun. About ten ladies are doing a very graceful circle dance. A wonderful organic trance-like state is happening, as if the purity of the music and dance is taking us back to the time when God walked the earth; yet it is now. The feeling is ... God has never really left.

A lady I'd talked to earlier, was sitting off to the side, and crying. We'd spoken of our mutual knee problems, and stretches and such, we could do to compensate. I went to see if I could help. After speaking briefly, I rubbed my Tiger Balm Oil on her knees. All her pain left. She told me later that the pain had been unbearable as she tried to sit on the floor. She felt that Swamiji had told her it was all right to sit in a chair. She knew that I would come over.

Swamiji says that Lord Datta is Deva Guru, Guru of the angels.

Swamiji says that once the Buddhi (intellect) thinks only of God and merges with the Atman (heart), then Moksha (liberation) occurs.

I took another container of holy water and a small plastic bookmarker with Swamiji's photo on it to Swamiji to be blessed. I said, "Jai Guru Datta." Swamiji blessed the objects but didn't say anything or look at me. Shortly after, as I reflected back, I was a little bothered by Sri Swamiji's non-attention. In a few hours, I realized that this was just my little ego, wanting attention, so I dropped it.

Back in Evansville, days later, I remembered that Sri Swamiji had moved Swamiji's head, slightly, side to side, as I was saying, "Jai Guru Datta."

This was a gesture I had heard of and seen previously. It's a subtle, often spontaneous, spiritual acknowledgment and attunement, a gesture that had happened to me, for the first time with clear true feeling, several times, those days in Baton Rouge ... a feeling of transcendence, or rising Kundalini, beyond physical or material limitations. Remembering this incident brings an inward smile (sometimes outward) and a blessing.

Walking back to the congregation, with my two newly blessed talismans, it came clearly to me that the bookmarker was meant for my friend from high school, who had helped finance my trip and volunteered to take care of my dog and bring in the mail.

I got to see Seema and Hina—it's been five years. I didn't recognize them initially, nor did they know me. I heard someone call Seema's name. I spoke to her briefly, reminding her of our past.

I remembered drawings the three of us had drawn in the back of my Kriya notebook. Initially, I didn't want to draw in the notebook, but they talked me into it. I felt then, that these drawings may mean more, later.

I mentioned the drawings to Seema, next time I saw her. Later, she came up to me to see them. The bond was coming back. Seema left saying, "Show it to Hina when she comes."—clearly implying Hina would also enjoy the drawings.

I showed the drawings to Hina. One was a portrait I'd done of her. We both knew that she should keep it.

We spoke of doing the Sikh walking chant.

I did some coin magic that I'd done for them before. Seema remembered me telling them how to do the tricks, just before leaving. I had forgotten that. My heart felt renewed.

July 12, 1995, it's Guru Poornima Day—the special day of the Guru, the Guru as Vyasa, the highest channel. This is the only time Swamiji has been in the United States on this day. We are all so blessed.

Swamiji says we are vibrations—that Swamiji is in us, that Swamiji is us.

There appears a great yogi, some fifteen feet above the devotees … sitting in full lotus, in blissful meditation. He is in a huge circular frame about twenty feet in diameter … with large snow topped mountains and clouds behind him. There is prana (movement) or snakes around his legs. He is a being of light, beyond our material dimension's limitations and pain. The feeling is … he has practiced for thousands of years. Is it Lord Shiva? The feeling is … pure … real … blissful … completely beyond the physical dimension.

I had done Tai Chi several times while there, to safely open my channels. I had felt several times before coming that Tai Chi was somehow connected to this gathering. The last time I did Tai Chi there, my legs felt rooted throughout the form, and the energy constantly flowed through my arms and back.

Swamiji returned to the United States in 1997. I was blessed

to see him in Baton Rouge, July 12–24. Considering the richness of each day, this is an extremely long time. One local organizer once told me that the week Swamiji stayed with him was more contact than he could have in a lifetime in India.

The bus ride down was very long, nineteen hours, and crowded. At least one person had very bad BO. Part of the way an attractive woman fell asleep leaning against me. Normally a pleasant thing, but since I was trying to sleep, this made it much worse. I could manage only about one hour's sleep, so arrived tired and stiff.

I was staying with Dinesh and Sejal Sthanki, who I'd also stayed with in 1990. Dinesh's mother was also staying with them. She once showed me their altar, saying that Goddess Amba gave her energy … I could feel the energy.

We got to the airport at 8:10 pm, Saturday, July 12, 1997, waiting for Swamiji's arrival at 9:10 pm. There were a lot more people greeting Swamiji at the airport. I met new people and saw faces I'd seen before. I saw Narendra Dave and Daulet Sthanki, Dinesh's brother. I talked to another of Dinesh's brothers, Lalit. Lalit was surprised I remembered his name.

Swamiji arrives. He greets everyone … touches me lightly on my shoulder. My legs are solidly grounded to the floor, with a smooth, subtle energy flowing through my body.

I spoke briefly with Smita Patel, a nice, young Indian lady who I'd first met in Evansville.

We went to the temple. It was very elevating, even though I was in the back.

In the car ride to Dinesh's we were chanting: *Om Aim Hreem Shreem Shiva Rama Anagha Datta Yanamaha.* I still chant this chant often.

I volunteered to help Dinesh with the janitorial work.

Sunday, July 13, 1997, I went for the morning Sri Chakra Puja (which Swamiji does every morning) and Homa (which Swamiji does every Sunday).

I was given a healing liquid from the Sri Chakra Puja. I drank some, and put the rest over my head and back. I felt the subtle textures of the liquid everywhere it touched me.

I'm given a talisman from the Sri Chakra Puja and a healing crystal on a string from the Homa.

I had nice talks with two lady devotees, one from Germany and one from Trinidad. I spoke again with Dr. Rao, the president of the Datta Yoga Center, USA. Dr. Rao is intelligent, friendly, and humble—the perfect personality for his position.

During the morning chanting of *Ashtalakshmi Stuthi*, I felt very clearly the sweet feminine essence of this chant—much more so than at any other time, before or since.

I also got to speak briefly with Radhakrishna and Prasad.

The evening *Namasankeertan* (chanting of the holy names of God), and discourse, were their usual elevation beyond words. As Swamiji walked past me to the stage, I was opening to his presence ... when he began to speak; I felt tears of joy welling up inside me. Twice, I briefly saw Swamiji's hand and arm as a solid green, as if of an elaborately carved idol.

Swamiji says: Only share problems with Sadguru because others have their own. ♦ Don't waste time, think of God/Guru. God is everywhere: stone, flower, river, doubt is God, all is God ... reach God. ♦ We are not serving Swamiji. Swamiji is serving us. ♦ "*Aim*" is knowledge. "*Hreem*" is harmony. "*Sreem*" is Laxshmi (wealth on all levels). ♦ Changes in life are to be accepted as calmly as the changes in the seasons. ♦ Pure love seeks nothing in exchange. Love of God should be motiveless. ♦ God is the only friend of yours in calamity and adversity; when you realize this, you will have peace and fearlessness. ♦ The Lord knows what you want. So you need not pray for favors. He is pleased only with your devotion and sincerity.

Seema waved to me sweetly as she left with Swamiji.

Swamiji is coming to Dinesh's at 9:00 am tomorrow for Pada Puja.

Monday, July 14, 1997, I filmed the Pada Puja at Dinesh's. Swamiji looked at me as I was filming, seemed to see that I was busy working, and then looked away.

I rested some in the temple, but foolishly lie down with my feet facing the altar. Someone points out my mistake. I thank her and immediately turn my feet away from the idols ... then receive a pleasant rush of energy, which settles into a subtle feeling of well being. My arms occasionally rise from the elbows with the palms facing the altar. Pleasing energy then flows into my hands and down the arms.

I met several people from my Kriya Yoga Class of 1988. Very interesting, as this is the first time I've been able to do much socializing with the other Americans. Ean was in that class. He spoke of some of the others. Sherry Hennie was the one who took photographs. I still have some of them. It was for such a short time, and so long ago. I'm unclear as to who was who—an awkward byproduct of these infrequent gatherings.

Dinesh says the mantra Swamiji used was "*So Ham*".

Tuesday, July 15, 1997, I start doing janitorial work today.

Nalini Dave came up to me and said, "Nice to see you." I replied, "Jai Guru Datta."

I find that I'm doing various subtle head gestures in dialogue with others, that I've never done before.

I bought the book, *Niti Mala*. Swamiji says this book is especially easy for New Age people to understand. I may have the actual book that Swamiji touched. I've since loaned it out to a few people.

Swamiji told a beautiful story where a man asked Swamiji how Swamiji could resist beautiful women. Swamiji then told him that angels are always with Swamiji and their beauty is much greater than humans. Swamiji then allowed the man to see one of the angels. The man motioned to touch the angel. Swamiji stopped him saying that they were use to Swamiji's touch and that his would be too harsh.

We went to the home of Lalit Sthanki in Lafayette, Louisiana. I filmed the Pada Puja there also. I was getting use to the zoom lens. Swamiji graciously accepted that I was working, and didn't look at me … an odd double edged sword, as I gained some respect, but lost the possibility of a direct physical healing.

The people there got one of the mantras wrong. Usually it's me not them.

I met a nice man from Nepal. He was surprised that I've actually met the Dalai Lama and some of the Dalai Lama's relatives. He went quickly to get his wife and kids. Then his family attentively listened as I told them of my experiences and knowledge of the Dalai Lama.

Wednesday, July 16, 1997, in the morning, I had a pleasant conversation with Sejal. Dinesh and I are both exhausted and will put some of our cleaning off, as long as we can.

Sejal is from Northern India and doesn't understand Swamiji's language. She said it would be best if I learned Swamiji's language—still on my list of things to do.

Dinesh's mother is called Da, which means mother. Sejal says Da likes me. Once in broken English, Da says that this is my family.

I just finished a meal with the ladies. I had a soup of potatoes, carrots, cashews, and mild spices; with rice/lentil patties that we tore into small pieces to put into the soup. The rice/lentil patties were soaked overnight and then steamed.

To the temple, first we wash our feet outside the temple, and then walk three times clockwise around the Audambara Tree (fig tree).

Inside, Swamiji walks past me, and my hands become welded together by a gentle warm healing energy. I even feel the energy, briefly, after I take my hands apart. When I put my hands back together, the energy returns.

A gentle, elderly priest named Subramunya comes up to me and says, "I'm from India." I answer, "I'm from Indiana." He then says, "Then we're brothers."

I talk some with Linda Heil about her concern about her daughter's ballet tomorrow night in the Cultural Program. I reassure her that Swamiji's in control.

Dinesh now has some other responsibilities, so I will be doing most of the janitorial work. I will also be the night watchman in the Bhavan (where the meals and most of the activities are held), because there is a lock but no key to the counter where the tapes/CDs/books/videos etc. are kept. So, the new plan is that Will Bertolette will pick me up between 6:15 am–7:00 am. Will, earlier, gave me a Sri Chakra watch that Radhakrishna had given him, when Will found out that I had no watch because mine had recently broken. At Will's, I'll bathe, eat breakfast, and come back to do my janitor work and participate in what activities I can fit in.

When Sejal says that's a lot for me to do, I mention that it's not work but Seva (holy service which is truly a blessing).

Swamiji holds up a large, beautiful, Dattatreya poster, saying this is something that'd be a blessing to have. I go to the bookstall and buy the same poster that Swamiji held—it's still on my altar.

There's another other-worldly Namasankeertan. The exquisite violinist even plays background when Swamiji speaks.

I got to speak some with Seema and Hina. Someone else came up and I referred to the girls as my nieces—the girls nodded affectionately in agreement.

Swamiji says that before going to bed we should pray to Datta to forgive our mistakes.

I can't lock up until everyone has left, and there are always devotees working late. The last people left at 1:56 am. They left a mess to clean up, but said they will come and do it in the morning. I'll probably do it, because I'll have to prepare for putting the clean sheets on the floor that we sit on when eating.

Several of the young boys talked to me just before they left. They were nice and intelligent. One brought me some ice packs, because he noticed I was having stiffness in my neck when I got up.

With everyone gone, I tried to meditate sitting on Swamiji's throne, but had to quit, because I wasn't sure if it was proper. I did have a good meditation looking at the large photo of Jayalaxshmi Mata, Swamiji's mother and guru.

Thursday, July 17, 1997, I woke refreshed, after less than two hours sleep, cleaned up after the late workers, put the white sheets down on the floor, emptied the trash, and cut the soap in half so there'd be soap in both restrooms.

Will picked me up, and then I went to his home to bathe. Will plays exquisite Jazz piano. Mickey and Stewart are also staying with Will. Mickey is originally from NW Indiana, and has worked in Silicon Valley. Stewart is from New Orleans, and has been a merchant seaman. The priest I'd spoken with, Subramunya, had stayed here last night. Driving back to the temple, we chanted *Datta Stava.* I was just getting use to it.

I met Jewell Branch. She was in my 1988 Kriya Yoga Class. We had spoken briefly in Narendra's home in 1988. She has been very active with Swamiji and has organization. She's very friendly and a marvelous story teller—I've learned a lot from her.

Swamiji said that twenty percent of the time we should serve others, and eighty percent of the time we should work on ourselves. He said we shouldn't select the spiritual field as our business.

I'm trying to get a private audience with Swamiji. Finally, I find out that Prasad is the main person to go through for this.

I met a lady pharmacist named Gita. She told me that Benadryl may work for my eggplant allergy. My doctor had given me a huge injection needle, but it's just too awkward to carry with me. These gatherings are the only times I worry about it, as eggplant is more frequently used in the Indian diet.

Seema and Hina are working as food servers in the food line, so I ask them if anything has eggplant. They say, "No."

The food didn't taste good. I developed a slight fever. After walking around a little, there was still a mild headache. I'm thinking that maybe it's because I didn't have much sleep.

Then I start getting very paranoid—this seems an irrational feeling in this holy environment. I follow a compulsion to go into the fresh air, and then to quickly walk away. I walk out of the industrial area onto a major road. I go into a McDonalds to eat and get my baring. Sitting there with a Coke and French fries, I'm getting much worse. I'm dizzy and feeling I may pass out. Then it hits me—eggplant! I anxiously look around. Miraculously, nearby is a drugstore. Using all the willpower I can muster, I make it to the drugstore and take the Benadryl. In a few minutes I'm back to normal.

Tonight is a Cultural Program. Nice music, dance, and skits from people of all ages. The last is a circle dance that's a folk dance from India. I had done it before. You move counter-clockwise, bend into the circle and clap downwards on a heavy beat, then clap with hands up, pointing outward, as you stand erect on a lighter beat. A trance state develops quickly. It starts with just a few ladies. I'm the first man to join. Now there are several rings with about fifty people. Swamiji comes into the middle, and beats out the rhythm on two wooden sticks. The joyful music is moving me effortlessly.

The dance ends, and I walk away through the crowd. An older Indian lady looks at me and says, "You dance nice."

Stewart also sleeps in the Bhavan this night.

Friday, July 18, 1997, I woke at 4:20 am, alert and with cleaning seva to do. I vacuumed some, cleaned Swamiji' throne, laid the floor sheets down, cleaned the bathrooms and meal serving area, and emptied the large trash can in the kitchen area.

This is the first of three days of the main rituals for this gathering. It's *Praana Prathishta*, breathing life into the idols. Because of my seva, I'll miss much of it.

At 7:05 am, I'm sitting outside in a cool morning breeze, waiting for Will. He came, then to his home, then back to the temple—we were running a little late. We got back just as Sri Chakra is starting. This happens a lot—hurrying is rarely justified.

I spoke some to Stewart.

I got another healing crystal from another Fire Ceremony. Swamiji handed it directly to me. It's amazing how little I know. Every fiber of my being tells me that this environment is the best that can be. Tensions dissolve and I'm more and more aware of what my deeper nature is. Joy and bliss permeate every particle and thought here. Mistakes are divine cleansings.

Swamiji says: Shiva means Yoga—grants wishes. ♦ Kali, Saraswati, and Laxshmi—all three are Laxshmi. ♦ Brahma means knowledge. ♦ Same Karma leads to sin or Moksha—same key, one way open, one close. ♦ Show the Sadguru the top of your head when you bow.

Narayane from Newburgh, Indiana, is here. He's published a book about Swamiji called "*God Word*".

I tried again to get a private audience with Swamiji, thought I was close today—I waited in the temple for hours—putting off some of my chores. When I finally had to accept that I wasn't getting an audience today, I hurried to try and catch up on my chores, but someone had already done them.

I sometimes had to recruit others to help—which was actually very easy. Once I had to get a truck and several strong men to move carpets from the Fire Ceremony to the Bhavan in a very short time. Daulat's son Manish was the biggest help.

I spoke briefly with Jackie Freeman's sister, Sandy. Sandy has a bar deep in the Bayou—deeper than most people realize that there is a bar. Many of the people there hunt for subsistence and barter. She's a wonderful story teller—except when it gets scary.

Writing this twelve years after it happened has some limitations. Sometimes my notes don't make sense. I have forgotten details. When I'm actively participating, I often don't want to, or can't take notes. When there's finally a quiet time, I may be tired or hungry. Each moment is incredibly rich. A book could be written on each day. It's magical to go back to these blessed times ... they become alive to me again.

Now, back to 1997, a yellow string is tied to my wrist, with a vow to be disciplined for these three holy days.

At the end of the night session, Swamiji called up someone with mental problems. Then gradually others started coming forward. Swamiji would direct one to four, or so, at a time. Swamiji would then touch them quickly (usually lightly on the third eye).

I hesitated, and then cautiously walked forward, as it seemed clear that there were people coming who didn't have big mental problems. Everyone wants Swamiji's blessing, but most are trying not to be greedy—it's a fine line.

Swamiji stopped others from queuing up, a few people behind me. As my turn came, Swamiji motioned to me to come and sit between the two people already there. I was pulled effortlessly to my spot. I came, bent forward, and Swamiji touched my third eye.

Years later, I was talking to someone who was one of the first ones called up. She seemed very stable. She told me that back then she wasn't, that she was in the middle of major life adjustments.

Saturday, July 19, 1997, I went to bed at 12:30 am, woke at 4 am, and did my seva. Every night I set my alarm clock, and wake up before it rings.

I got a healing crystal from the mornings Ganapati Homa. Swamiji handed it to me directly. I will take these talisman's blessed by Swamiji, back to Evansville, and then put them on my altar, creating a holy environment in my home.

Swamiji said that Swamiji could heal us directly, but what would happen to our Karma's—that is why pujas and rituals are necessary.

The only thing that Swamiji signs are copies of his large autobiography. He's looking to sign one but there is no pen. Someone comes to me and borrows my pen. I wait and watch. Many others come to have Swamiji bless some object or sign his book. Then Swamiji leaves. My pen is left on his throne. I get the pen, wrap some tape around it, and write something on it. I use it for several days ... I seem to write clearer. Then I lose it.

Swamiji does miracles. The most common is manifesting small objects. People excitedly follow Swamiji out of the kitchen. I hear that Swamiji has just manifested a Shiva Linga, while saying to the cooks that they are cooking something other than food. I walk into the crowd and see Swamiji reach one hand into his other hand, which holds something like curried rice. Swamiji pulls out another Shiva Linga.

A sweet little girl of about nine has been following me around for several days. Once she grabbed my arm and wouldn't let me cross the street. She asked me if she was bugging me. Of course, I said, "No." After the Namasankeertan she quickly came up to me and hugged my leg. I patted her on the head.

I did my coin magic tricks for two other little girls, who I met several days ago with their mother at Dinesh and Sejal's. I showed the older one how to do some of it. The younger one came up to me today, and said that her sister stayed up most of the night practicing the tricks.

I got to speak more with Ruth, the woman from Trinidad. Trinidad has, for a long time, been a fantasy place for me to visit, so I'm fascinated when I meet someone from there. Ruth is a recently divorced high level government official. She says it's difficult to meet single men that aren't intimidated by her position. She tells me of Dadaji, an elderly Indian man that I had already noticed. People approach Dadaji timidly and respectfully. Ruth says that Dadaji knew Mahatma Gandhi, and that his stories are fascinating.

Later, I'm sitting alone in the Bhavan. Dadaji is sitting directly, some fifty feet, in front of me. I occasionally glance his way. Finally, he's sitting alone. I walk up to him, bow respectfully, and say that I had heard that he had met Gandhi, and would love to hear anything about Gandhi that he felt comfortable sharing. Then begins some of the most interesting stories I have ever heard. Dadaji refers to Gandhi as Gandhiji. Dadaji is highly educated and extremely articulate. He has met Gandhiji three times. The first was when Dadaji was in school—the equivalent of our tenth grade. Gandhiji came to Dadaji's school to hand out awards—Dadaji was given one for History.

The second time was in the famous salt march. Gandhiji was defying the British by marching to the sea to make salt. The British had told the Indians that they had to buy their salt from them.

The third time was when Gandhiji was giving a speech. In the speech Gandhiji was talking against anyone being considered untouchable. Outside were protesters with black flags, which meant that they were against Gandhiji's opinion. Some of the protesters got too close and were beaten by Gandhiji's followers. Gandhiji rushed to the entrance of the hall and stopped the violence. Gandhiji said that he was ashamed of his followers, and told them that as penance they must fast for three days ... and because it happened in his presence, he would also fast.

Someone told me later that Dadaji had been a railroad official, and that when stationed in a poor village, he started a school there with his own money.

I did more seva and spoke with others, including Jewel.

I heard miraculous stories of Swamiji's birth and who he really is. Hard to believe, but when you experience miracles, you know that anything's possible. I briefly saw Swamiji's hand as transparent.

Sunday, July 20, 1997, Guru Purnima, the full moon worship where the guru's blessings are easier to attain.

I got to bed at 3:30 am, woke at 6:00 am, and did my seva.

Waiting for Swamiji, I put my meditation shawl on and accidentally strike the glasses of the man next to me. I say, "I'm sorry." He replies, "That's alright—nothing hurts here."

I had a very pleasant conversation with Maunica Sthanki, Daulat's daughter. One of the things we spoke of was my writing. It was announced that it was time to bring our gifts to Swamiji. I felt embarrassed, as I had no money left. Maunica suggested I write Swamiji a poem. I sat down, and a poem just flew through my hand. I tried to keep a copy of it, but have lost the copy.

Swamiji gave us this mantra: *Om Aim Hreem Shreem Namahshivaaya.* Swamiji says it is for desires, money problems, family problems, and business problems. Swamiji Says, "Don't say you know this mantra. This is a Upadesha to you, and Swamiji has chanted this for you on this day—Guru Purnima Day. It is important. It is Guru Kripa."

Monday, July 21, 1997, I attend the morning Sri Chakra Puja. Sometimes a flame is held high in the air, towards the congregation. People lift their hands up with palms facing the flame, and then put their hands on their eyes and/or over the top of their heads. I started doing this also and sometimes can even feel the heat from the flame.

I loaned my pen to Nitya to write down her date to sponsor a puja.

A man sitting near me was looking through a purse he thought was his wife's. When he discovered it wasn't, he apologized, blushed, and went further back to sit. Some devotees laughed and joked about this.

An Indian woman was explaining to Nitya (an American) how happy she was with the process of getting an arranged marriage for her child.

Some of the things Swamiji said today: Where the woman is respected, go to that city and live there. ♦ I'm nectar and poison—no difference. ♦ Jayalaxshmi, Swamiji's mother, gave away millions in jewels when Swamiji was born. ♦ Swamiji was a ritual beggar. Swamiji knows poor people. ♦ Swamiji materialized a Goddess for a scientist. ♦ This is Lila, God's play. If you want to cry, cry. If you want pain, work hard. ♦ I'm observing rules for your sake. ♦ I'm Agni (fire). ♦ The real miracles are: we're here, alive, have good mind, and are positive. ♦ There's a young boy here who can do miracles.

Finally, I got my private audience with Swamiji. A few days earlier, I had a message through Radhakrishna about my earlier writings. Swamiji said that I should include more details, say more about Swamiji, and that because of the drug references the Ashram wouldn't publish it, as is, but I was free to publish it commercially.

My first question to Swamiji was if I should accept a ride to Datta Retreat Center in West Sunbury, Pennsylvania, where Swamiji is scheduled to be soon. It would be with a German lady named Mauna, and an American Indian lady named Laura. Swamiji put both hands in the air, with palms facing me, and then shook his hands while saying, "No." Well, that was clear.

Swamiji then said, "Is there anything else?" Of course, there were a thousand questions I could ask, but in his presence it's difficult to speak. Partly because problems dissolve, and partly because you realize that compared to Swamiji's level, most of us aren't even qualified to ask a question. I reply, "Is there anything that Swamiji ... ah?", as I'm waving my hands in a shaky manner, indicating my uncertainty. Swamiji says, "We'll keep communicating through thoughts."

Now it comes to the question I really wanted to ask, and had been preparing for, for months. During this period, Swamiji kept a bowl full of healing crystals beside him during the private audiences, and when the audience was over, Swamiji would give each person one crystal. Well, I wanted ten crystals. I had never seen, or heard, of anyone getting more than one. I was working with some at-risk children, and felt these crystals could benefit them. I tried to honestly reflect, to be sure there was no ego or greed in my request. Reflecting on the families I was working with, there were three siblings that I had very little direct contact with, so, that left ten who I clearly had direct input into their lives.

So, when it came to when Swamiji was reaching for the crystal, I told him that I was working with at-risk children and would like ten crystals. Swamiji began slowly counting the crystals out one-by-one. He says, "That's ten, right?" I say, "Yes." Then again he says, "You said ten?" I say, "Yes, Swamiji." My trance state is now even more heightened than usual ... I'm in a higher state of awareness, one I rarely reach. Yet, I don't understand why Swamiji keeps asking me the number of crystals that I want. Then again Swamiji says, "You said ten?" I reply, "Yes, Swamiji." Swamiji hands me the crystals. I walk out, sit down, and count the crystals ... there are thirteen!

A little later, I saw Kali Ray standing by herself. She's an American devotee who's known for her gift of communicating with Swamiji through thought. This had happened to me clearly a few times, but, there were other times when I wasn't sure. Since Swamiji told me today that we'd keep communicating through thoughts, I thought that Kali Ray may help me decipher which thoughts are coming from Swamiji.

I had seen Kali Ray at other gatherings, so she probably, at least, knew me by sight. I walked up to her, introduced myself, and asked her advice on how to tell if we're receiving Swamiji's thoughts. She replied that the thoughts would be Satvic in nature. One could feel his presence, peace, tingling, light, or energy movement. She said, "It's nice to meet you." I found our dialogue helpful.

At night I cleaned my meditation shawl and hung it up to dry—a daily ritual. Only two-thirds of the carpet is swept, and I don't know where the vacuum cleaner is or if it's fixed.

Tuesday, July 22, 1997, I'm up at 3:30 am. Did come cleaning, and then Will came. At his place, I did a quick laundry, ate a few oranges, and skimmed the daily newspaper. Will has this great soap that I keep forgetting to ask him what it's called.

The mantra, *Om Aim Hreem Shreem Namahshivaaya,* is pleasantly going through my mind.

I spoke with Jewell and Shawn, a fifteen, year old who has been to India with Swamiji.

After the Sri Chakra, I'm sitting in the temple. Swamiji, Dr. Rao, and Radhakrishna are talking on the stage. I hear Swamiji say, "Mr. Roberts can do it." I stand up so they can see me. Radhakrishna motions for me to sit down.

Swamiji says that at a concert in India, a crystal rose into the air, moved over, then dropped and broke. He says that's because it was absorbing karmas. He says that when a crystal points upward it releases karma upward.

Swamiji says that it is very foolish to spend a lot of money on a thread ceremony.

Swamiji will leave tomorrow, a day early. My bus leaves tomorrow at 2:30 pm.

Wednesday, July 23, 1997, I do my morning seva for the last time. Sri Chakra Puja starts late, as everyone is packing to leave. After the Sri Chakra, I wait in line for my talisman, watching to see what the procedure is this time. I give my sponsorship card to Ramesh, and bow before Swamiji. When coming up from paying my respects, Swamiji smiles at me. I get my talisman from the violin player, and go back to my seat.

There aren't many of us left. Swamiji says to use a blue light when meditating on Dattatreya.

I speak briefly with Bindu, an American, lady devotee.

I leave with Jewel. We go to a gazebo in a botanical park, next to a building where she gave her first Ayurveda (Eastern medicine) lecture. We have a wonderful talk, and then she takes me to the bus station. We write often and meet at future gatherings.

Swamiji came back to the United States in 1998. This time there was a Sri Chakra Puja at Sudheer and Mythili Gurram's home in Newburgh, Indiana, and a Namasankeertan and discourse session at the Holiday Inn in Evansville. The Holiday Inn is within walking distance of my home, and I'm excited about the possibility of getting Swamiji's blessing for many of the people I know.

Friday, 8:30 am, July 3, 1998, is the Sri Chakra Puja at the Gurram's. I went with my sister Linda and great-niece Crystal White.

The home was very crowded. I knew most of the Americans that came: Carey Smith and his daughter, Stacy; Jackie Freeman and her sister, Sandy; sisters, Shelly and Michelle Sides; Anna Horton and her boyfriend Bryan; Ruth Hetzel; Mary Beth Davis; Jann Thomas; and Diane Arneson. Others, who I knew their face or just their first names, were also there.

The Sri Chakra was its usual elevating and calming influence. Linda and Crystal got the blessed talismans from the Sri Chakra. Then these beautiful, multi-colored, healing necklaces were sold. They are to be worn for a maximum of one or two hours a day, and not to be slept with. They are for chronic illness. Crystal asked Linda for one. Linda told her that she didn't have a long term illness. Crystal said that it was for the future—so, she got one.

I got to speak some with Kali Ray.

That night Swamiji was at the Holiday Inn in Evansville. I talked to as many people as I could, who I thought would be ready for this experience. Then I went to the home of Kristina and Nikki Nation. I was happy to get these two little girls to go. I had known them since they were very small and lived next door. Over the years, psychic occurrences had happened between us. Four kids at their home, who I hadn't met before, also came: Johnny, Kacy, and a brother and sister, Lewis and Andrea. We wound up getting there an hour late.

Swamiji did a lot of talking, as there were a lot of first-timers there. The acoustics weren't good. One person who was very impressed was Diane Arneson. She asked me to tell her when Swamiji returns.

I was happy to see my Christian minister friend, Joe Ferguson. He's a scholar, who is also open, perceptive, and kind. He's preached in Israel, and one year was given a small chip off of the rock that Jesus was crucified on.

Also there was Mel Meinschein. He's known locally as "The Bird Man" as he has parakeets he's trained.

I was very happy that my old friend Paul Allyn came. Paul is the only local person I know who has been into yoga longer than me. He's a retired railroad detective, has been to India, and had a private audience with the Dalai Lama. Paul also has been a long-time student of Roy Eugene Davis, a direct disciple of Paramahansa Yogananda. I watched as he waited in line for his turn to approach Swamiji. This was usually a very brief greeting, ending with Swamiji giving them a healing crystal.

But when it was Paul's turn, Paul and Swamiji clasped each other's hands like old friends. This really shouldn't have surprised me, as Paul is one of the most honest and genuinely caring people I've ever met, yet he is also strong and wise. This was the first time Paul met Swamiji.

Most of the people from this morning's Sri Chakra came. Ana Horton gave Swamiji her card and invited Swamiji to visit her. She spoke appropriately and respectfully.

Saturday, July 4, 1998, Swamiji went to St. Louis. I traveled there in Carey Smith's comfortable van with Carey and his daughter Stacy, sisters Shelly and Michelle Sides, and Heath. They all had seen Swamiji in Evansville.

It was at the same temple as in 1990—there were a lot of wonderful idol consecration ceremonies, but Swamiji wasn't directly involved in most of it. Swamiji did do Namasankeertan upstairs in the Mahatma Gandhi Center in front of the temple—another elevating session.

Later, walking around among the festivities, an American devotee came up to me and told me that Swamiji would be doing Homa at a home nearby. She gave me the address and directions. I quickly found my traveling companions. Only Heath wanted to go. We searched for the site. One street was off of an intersection at a sharp angle—we got lost twice. I convinced the others that it was still worth it, even though we would be late. Finally, we pulled up to the home. Homa was in an open garage, overflowing with some two hundred people. It had just ended. Swamiji was giving out healing crystals from the Homa. Usually you have to pay ten dollars for one, and do it before the Homa starts. Swamiji said that this time everyone here gets a crystal. And that these crystals are unique in that they are to be used when bathing, whereas with others it's the opposite. There was a great outdoor meal. In this environment food digests better. We had just eaten several hours earlier, but were again hungry and easily digested the second meal.

Heath went to the bookstall to buy a book. The clerk and I agreed on which book would be best for him—he bought *Niti Mala*.

We met an impressive woman who was helping American Indians in the Northwest.

Our pit stop coming back to Evansville was Applebee's Restaurant in Mt. Vernon, Illinois.

In 1999 Swamiji returned to the United States—this time just to Baton Rouge and California. Just six days before Swamiji was to arrive, it didn't seem as though I would have Swamiji's Darshan this time. I had a long meeting I couldn't miss on September 11th. Swamiji was due to arrive in Baton Rouge late on the ninth and leave early on the thirteenth. I had no car and no money.

Then on September fourth I received a letter saying my appointment was cancelled. I called to confirm the cancellation and left a phone message with a man with an Indian accent. Feels like Swamiji has again arranged for me to have his Darshan. Jeanie Knight volunteered to drive ... so, we were off.

We left Friday night, September 10, 1999, at 6:00 pm. We drove for thirteen hours, throughout the night. The drive was magical as new melody variations of common mantras spontaneously flowed through me.

September 11, 1999, we arrived in Baton Rouge just in time to check into our hotel and make the morning festivities at the temple. We were staying at Motel 6, which was just two miles from the temple. The temple was very crowded. I sat next to Padma. She didn't recognize me—it wasn't 'till the next day that I realized that this was the first time I'd been around Swamiji without a beard. As I age, it's more convenient to look conservative. Wonderful mantras and purification rituals by Swamiji and the other priests relaxed and centered us. Swamiji said that the United States devotees were lucky, because the visit was almost cancelled, and was later fixed as Swamiji had to attend a function in California.

We went back to the hotel to nap before the evening events.

Sri Chakra Puja was performed at 6:30 pm—it's usually done in the morning.

Sunday, September 12, 1999, was a Maha Ganapati festival—it's worship and attunement to Ganapati, the elephant God, who is the remover of obstacles. Sri Swamiji performed Abhishekam (ritual cleansing) to the Ganapati idol consecrated in the temple. The priests chanted the Ganapati Sukta and Ganapati Atharva Sheersha. I sat close to Bindu and spoke with her briefly.

From there we went into the Bhavan where Sri Chakra Puja and Siddhi Vinayaka Vratam were performed. We were given plates with offering items to perform Siddhi Vinayaka Vratam to Lord Ganapati. We were instructed in mantra use and hand mudras (held positions). Afterwards we were given Modakam (a favorite sweet of Lord Ganapati), directly from Swamiji.

Jeanie fully participated, and was respectful. It's rewarding and up-lifting to me, to play a small part in someone's spiritual growth.

Thursday, July 6, 2000, 8:30 pm, Jeanie Knight and I left Evansville for Chicago to see Swamiji. We arrived at the Radisson O'Hare Hotel in the middle of the night, and set an early wake-up call to make the morning's Sri Chakra Puja.

Friday, July 7, 2000, we made it on time to the Mahalaxmi Hall inside the Manav Seva Mandir in the Chicago suburb of Bensenville. After the Sri Chakra Puja was over Swamiji unveiled a portrait of Jayalakshmi Mata (Swamiji's holy mother). Swamiji then released a beautiful, large souvenir booklet for this leg of Swamiji's tour.

This was the first time that I'd been to this temple. During the break, before the evening program, we went into the temple proper where the idols are kept. We met some of the devotees and had them take photos of us.

In the evening, we attended a Namasankeertan session in the opulent Chicago Symphony Orchestra Hall. Over a thousand people were there. We purchased the most expensive tickets, so we would be close enough to receive a blessing, and maybe have some direct contact with Swamiji. At one point in the concert, Swamiji went walking down the aisles. He touched me on the shoulder as he passed. He also touched, at least, one other person. Swamiji's music was at its usual unexplainable depth. Leaving, we're more alive, yet centered and calm.

Driving back to the hotel, we got caught in a horrible traffic jam. It took us several hours to travel the seventeen miles. I had told Jeanie how bad it could be, but she didn't believe me—now she does. Later, we heard that a pop concert ended as we were leaving our concert.

Saturday and Sunday's events were all in the Mahalaxmi Hall. Sri Chakra Puja and Niti Mala lectures were in the morning. Darshan and Niti Mala lectures were in the evening. The Niti Mala lectures are from Swamiji's book that he says is like a modern Bhagavad Gita. All of the lectures were in Hindi, but it really doesn't matter, as the energy is the same. Sometimes, it even seems better to me, as my intellect is neutralized, allowing my higher self to emerge.

There were nice snacks, but one time I ate too much. I had to leave to go to the bathroom during the program—a stupid waste of precious time with Swamiji.

Thursday, June 26, 2003, I left by bus to see Swamiji in Baton Rouge, Louisiana. I always try to sit in the front, because the less rowdy people usually sit there. I feel Swamiji's guidance and presence when preparing to go, but once the journey actually starts, it's even more intense. I'm open to Swamiji's guidance and presence in all the people and circumstances I incur on the journey, both there and back.

From Evansville to Nashville was unique and sometimes even frightening. The driver was fairly new. This was a route she'd yet to drive, and there had been recent changes. She had a printout, with portions crossed out in ink, and rewritten. In places, it was difficult to read. I was just casually talking to her, and didn't jump in until she left a small town going due west, when we were supposed to be going southeast. Turning the huge bus around on a small country road wasn't easy. In one small town, I had to find a man sitting in the back, who had actually lived in that town, to come up front and guide us through. We arrived in Nashville two hours late. I missed my connection and had to wait another hour and a half for another bus. Most of the passengers agreed that we were just happy to get there alive.

I had a nice, long conversation at the bus station in Nashville with a man who had just left the Abbey of Gethsemani. He's a follower of the Christian mystic, Thomas Merton.

June 27, 2003, 6:10 pm, I arrived in Baton Rouge. The scheduled arrival was 2:20 pm. I then took a cab to Motel 6, which is the closest hotel to the temple.

The next morning, June 28, 2003, I went to the Sri Chakra Puja and discourse with Jewel and Sri Maatha, a nice lady from California, who I had met here in a previous year. During Sri Chakra Puja, I felt a blissful energy along my spine about the size of my little finger. It lasted for about ten minutes.

I went to the evening Namasankeertan at Louisiana State University's Union Theater in Baton Rouge with Jewel and Sri Maatha. Sri Narendra Dave, who first brought Swamiji to Baton Rouge in 1988, lit the inaugural lamp. The musicians are warming up. Prasad is playing synthesizer—this is the only time I've heard him play. I mention to Jewel, "They're better warming up than most popular musicians actually performing." She laughs. I ramble on with Jewel, talking somewhat nervously on various subjects.

The other-worldly concert begins. I did Kundalini Yoga during a back and joint healing raga. Just at the moment I'm trying to connect to Swamiji, he turns and looks directly at me. I don't feel as high during the concert, as I've usually felt at other concerts; but after this one, I'm floating in another dimension, and the world is perfect.

Sunday, June 29, 2003, this morning's Sri Chakra Puja was incredible, even though I was in pain and hadn't slept much. I could see Sahasrar Chakra better than only one other time. I saw parts of Swamiji's arm in deep green with engravings—this happened about seven times, but only lasted for a second each time. Swamiji performed Arati after Tailabhisheka to the idols of Ganapathy, Datta and Anagha, and Shiva.

I spoke briefly with Mukunda, the husky guy who was staying with Will in 1997, when I also stayed there. He had to remind me of his spiritual name.

I met two people from my Kriya Yoga Class of 1988—Danyel, who I had spoken to some in 1988, and her mother Divena, who was also in that class. Danyel has a smile that makes her look younger and my heart feel younger. Both women had been to Egypt. Divena introduced me to two of her friends. One's name was Heidi. We agreed that we should meet more than once every fifteen years.

I also got to talk more with Ean from that Kriya Yoga Class. Ean seems to know more about the people from that class, than anyone else. It's fascinating to hear more of what has happened to people after Swamiji's Darshan—particularly from an initiation. The great blessing that we've all received, surely, must have given us all a bigger boost, than we would have had without it.

I also met a Christian nun who was there for the first time. We spoke of Thomas Merton.

Jewel was short-changed at the bookstall. She paid with a hundred and was given change for a fifty. I went with her as she complained. The young girl said there were no hundreds. I pointed out to her, one sticking out under some smaller bills. She gave the correct change, but never apologized or admitted her mistake.

I had felt the power and bliss of *Astalaksmi Stuti* more consistently at this gathering than any other.

Many people gave Swamiji flowers that were then put on the side of the stage. I was asked to put these flowers into two large vases that sat in front of the stage. The shriveled flowers, I threw away. The others I cut to fit into the vases. There was time pressure, as Swamiji was coming soon. Several people volunteered to help me. It went smoothly and artistically.

After Sri Chakra Puja, Seetha Rama Kalyanam (symbolic marriage) was performed. The idols came from Mysore, India. Daulat Sthanki, who had donated the temple land, donated more land next to the

Jayalaxmi Bhavan. Dr. Rao mentioned the need of building a Guru Nilayam (residence for the guru).

Seema and Hina danced briefly with Swami Manasa, who was Radhakrishna, at the evening Namasankeertan.

I received a healing stone that was on a metal roller. I didn't hear the early discussion of it, but did pick up that you first immerse it in average water (not hot), and then gently, and slowly, roll it over the area, including the teeth and gums. I've been using it more lately.

Linda Heil gave me a ride back to my hotel. Her spiritual name is Tunga. Two young girls were with us. The girls told me their spiritual names—it was very sweet. I said, "I'm in the presence of three Goddesses." Tunga said, "You're very kind."

Monday, June 30, 2003, I attended rituals and chanting at the temple. Most of the devotees have left, or, are in the last stages of packing. The temple priests led a great chanting session.

I felt that I had less direct contact with Swamiji this time. I'm feeling disappointed, but catch myself; for it's a blessing just to be here.

I decided to stay on an extra day, because my bus was due to leave at the same time and place that Tropical Storm Bill was due to hit land. Also my path home would have been the same as the storm's path. That extra night was very clear and fresh, after the storm passed. I went looking for some food for my return trip, but was guided to the temple. I don't know if anyone will be at the temple, or even if it will be open. Only a few cars are there. I wash my feet and circumambulate the Audumbara Tree. A nice Indian lady tells me that Swamiji had just entered the temple, and was leaving soon with the musicians. I walk into the temple and stop as Swamiji enters through a side door. I respectfully put my hands in Namaskar as Swamiji approaches. Upon reaching me, Swamiji smiles and embraces my hands … I have my blessing.

A tall American devotee is in tears. I turn my head from her, or, I will also cry.

Monday, July 7, 2003, Swamiji comes back to Evansville/Newburgh.

The morning of July 8, 2003, there's Sri Chakra Puja at the Gurram's home in suburban Newburgh. My sister, Linda, drops me off slightly before it is due to start at 8:00 am. Then I'm told that it won't start until 9:00 am.

I decide to use this free time to meditate. I find a comfortable couch, sit, and then close my eyes. Sitting near me on the floor are about fifty people. I'm drawn strongly to one of the people and can't meditate. She's a woman I haven't met but may have seen before. I sit beside her and introduce myself. She's a professional psychic named Lou Wright. I explain to her some of the cultural differences, including specifics on how to have direct contact with Swamiji. Sometimes her mannerisms are like that of a Southern Belle.

After the Sri Chakra Puja, we go outside for a meal on picnic tables under a large tent. I point out Swami Manasa to Lou. She leaves me to talk with him. Jann Thomas gives me a ride back to Linda's. Bill Kempf is with us.

There was a concert scheduled that night at Deaconess Hospital. Sometimes finding Swamiji is referred to as hide-and-seek, so I checked the newspaper for any last second changes. There, in small print, was the change to Wheeler Concert Hall at the University of Evansville. This was particularly disheartening to me, because of all the direct contact I'd had with the local organizers. I contacted everyone that I could reach, who would probably be interested. I thought that surely they would contact Mary Beth Davis, who is on the staff of Deaconess Hospital and arranged the scheduled venue there. Just to be sure, I called Mary Beth—she hadn't been notified.

I'm usually aware that no matter what happens, it all works out even better than I had expected. This time is not an exception. I went to the concert early with Linda, my precious eight-year old great-niece Kristen White, and Hannah Marshal, a nine-year old neighbor of Kristen's. Kristen has done yoga with me several times, and feels it working quicker than most adults. We're blessed to be the first ones there, so get the choicest seats. I'm sitting in the middle of the front row. Kristen is to my left and Hannah beside her. Coming in shortly to sit next to Hannah is my teenage great-nephew, Thomas White. Behind me sits my brother Don. None of these people have had Swamiji's Darshan before. I am already satisfied, as it has been a long-time wish of mine to have more of my relatives have Swamiji's Darshan. To Don's left is Linda, and next to Linda are two of her friends, Connie and Ervin Conrad.

The concert hall fills and the speakers begin. Gonuguntla Lakshminarayana gives a welcoming speech. Sri Gurram Sudhir gives a vote of thanks for Swamiji coming. Dr. Prakasha Rao talks of Guru Tattva. Swami Manasa explains his understanding of Swamiji's music.

Swamiji speaks of the elephant God, Ganapathy. Ganapathy is Omkara, the primordial sound. Ganapathy is the formless invisible God. Swamiji sings: *"Gana Gana Gana Gana Ganapathy."*

Swamiji speaks of God as feminine and sings a mother Goddess bhajan: *"Sri Maata Maam Paatu."*

Swamiji says that there are many Gods because each person is unique. Each has his own ideas and wisdom, his own ways of thinking. So, Indian Gods are various, to match the individual requirements.

Swamiji says that just sitting in meditation is not enough—that we need exercise, social service, and chanting.

Swamiji says that shaving your hair is offering your ego.

He says that tears of happiness come from the far corners of the eyes, and sorrow tears come from the near corners.

Swamiji sings other Namasankeertans, and then the percussionists, Mridangist Shankar Ramesh and Tablist Mahesh Bhatt are highlighted.

I keep the tempo the way the Indians do by alternating palm-to-palm with back-of-hand to palm. I show this to Kristen to get her more attentive. She's still talking to Hannah some, so, I take her hand and do the beat with her. She gets it, and is now doing it on her own. It's very cute, and her timing is actually good. I feel something, look up, and Swamiji is smiling at Kristen … a blessed moment that makes all of my efforts worthwhile.

There are some questions. Swamiji says that his music cannot be classified. He says that we are in a dynamic life, which causes us to loose lot of energy. Music stills the mind and the musical vibrations affect the energy field around you and refresh it. The bottom line is it helps you to be peaceful.

We had to leave a little early, to get the girls home.

Also there were: Julia Wilkie, Lou Wright, Jann Thomas, Mary

Beth Davis, Carey Smith, Missy and Danny Knight, Diane Arneson, and Bill Kempf. Those were just the ones that I knew, and noticed at the time.

Tuesday, July 29, 2003, at 6:45 pm, I left Evansville by bus for Memphis. Swamiji will be there during the Paanch Aahnika Skanda Maha Yajna. Skanda is a brother of Lord Ganesh and is eternal youth. Skanda also grants knowledge and wealth. He helps overcome the sin of developing friendship with those who are unworthy. I'll be staying with my brother Wayne. This time I am blessed to be one of the sponsors. This is, of course, good Karma, but I also may get some extra blessed talismans and have a better seat.

Wednesday, July 30, 2003, at 1:15 am, I arrived in Memphis. Wayne picked me up at the bus station.

In the morning, I had a nice talk with Wayne's boy Mark. Mark has had health problems, but is open, honest, and perceptive—I always enjoy speaking with him. I told Mark of Swami Jyoti's meditation where you just think/feel: *I am bliss, I always have been bliss, and I always will be bliss.* Mark sat beside me on the couch reading Swamiji's news magazine, *Bhakti Mala.*

I also went for a walk with Wayne, his dog Marlene, and Wayne's other son, Reid, with Reid's dog Dixie. Reid is also very likeable. I mentioned that Dixie is the perfect name of a dog from the South.

The first day's events at the temple start at 4:30 pm. Wayne will drop me off at 3:30 pm and pick me up at the end. I always invite my Memphis relatives, but, as yet, none have come. But Wayne has started calling us a religion not a cult, so, there is a little progress.

At the temple, I met Dr. Prasad Duggirala, the temple president and the person I had communicated with about becoming a sponsor. He told me that a Yajna is a fire ritual for contacting a specific deity and this time it's Skanda. He says that Swamiji will be a little late, as his plane was late. That tonight's activities are all in the temple but future ones will be under the tent. Tonight the priests are given permission and the ability to perform the Yajna.

I got a nice hug from Swami Manasa. Saw Dr. Rao. The temple has many beautiful idols. While bowing my head in the temple, my head felt soft and pliable.

I had a multi-level conversation with an Indian man named Ram Gollamudi. He's retired and from Memphis. He went on a forty temple tour of India, and is reading the Bhagavad Gita.

I also spoke to an Indian boy who was born in Bangalore, India. He says that in India it's difficult to even get close to a Yajna.

I was given Prasad (blessed food) from a ritual, and then a large headdress was placed on my head, as it was with others there.

A yellow thread was tied to my wrist for sponsoring the Yajnam. With it, I took a vow that during this Yajna I will: only eat Satvic food, sleep on a hard surface, be celibate, not leave, no meat, no smoking, and no alcohol.

Swamiji arrived and had the Darshan of the main temple deity, Prasanna Venkateswara Swami, and then the other deities. Swamiji was briefed about the temple activities. Swami Manasa gave his usual scholarly and heart-felt introductory speech. Swamiji blessed the Yajna Vastras for the main priests. Swamiji is here because of Sri Duggirala Prasad (Dr. Prasad).

Tomorrow starts at 9:30 am.

Thursday, July 31, 2003, Wayne woke me at 8:30 am. I showered quickly and we were off to the temple.

There I met Gert Leerdam (Sadasiva) from Holland. He said he had trouble with my accent.

Swamiji arrived at the Yajna Shala (place where yajnas are performed) for performing the initial pujas for this Skanda Maha Yajna. The ceremonial fire was lit by churning of wood along with chanting of Vedic mantras. The fire was placed in the main Homa Kunda. The yajnas in five Homa Kundas continued till 1:00 pm. Then Sri Chakra was performed in the temple.

This poem came to me:

"One Day at the Temple"

In this rarified environment with the Sadguru,
    my complex problems melt into simple solutions.
The perfection of my limitations,
    cruise effortlessly over my mind's eye.

The natural joy of being in the present,
    pushes my illusionary plans into the background.
I thankfully sit here,
    vowing that I will never again:
forget the God's who are always here,
or reject the joy no matter how deep the pain.

I met a very interesting woman, Luxmih Forbes. She met Swamiji while interviewing him for her own TV show in Lakeland, Florida, in 1992. She's now living in Japan, and was born in Rhodesia. She says that Rhodesia no longer exists, and is replaced by a black hole called Zimbabwe. She's writing a book. We exchanged addresses and e-mails. She has inspiring faith and courage, yet is gentle and kind.

The evening Namasankeertan begins. Swamiji sings beautiful compositions inspired by the temple deities. Swamiji explains how each deity has his own vehicle who is trying to merge with him. That everything in a temple has a purpose. That it all is to ward off all inauspicious vibrations.

Back at Wayne's, I had another nice visit with Mark. Mark was playing his video football game while we talked. He told me how to play the game. He also spoke of his friends, his music, and that the best thing he'd ever done was create his daughter, Shanleigh.

Friday, August 1, 2003, at 8:20 am, I'm back at the temple. I got to speak more with Ram Gollamudi. He graciously explained to me, some details about each individual idol. Ram is in the spiritual stage of life.

Swamiji said to me, "Happy homa?" I replied, "Oh, yes." Because of my sponsorship, I am blessed to sit close to one of the Homa Kundas and throw a small offering into the fire with each repetition of the Skanda mantra: *Aim Hreem Sreem Klim Om Sauhu Saravana Bhava Swaha.* The fire is very hot, and sometimes smoke gets in my eyes. My back was hurting from the start, and I didn't think that I could sit on the hard floor for over half an hour, but because of the wonderful healing energy, I sat for over ten hours, relatively pain free.

Swamiji came into the Yajna Shala and went near each Homa Kunda.

Swamiji performed Sri Chakra Puja. I got holy water and three talismans from the Sri Chakra ... Swamiji smiled at me. One specific talisman, I felt was meant for my friend Sheila Silvia, so saved it for her.

Swamiji spoke of the Vedas, Puranas, Brahmins, and spiritual dance. He then said that the quality of a man's life depended on his following spiritual understanding. Swamiji is pleased with this Skanda Yajna.

I got to speak more with Sadasiva and Luxmih. Luxmih told a story where she was becoming very ill while waiting in line in India, and after praying to Swamiji, a powerful man rushed to her and moved her to the front. Another time a girlfriend and her felt like avoiding a concert, but were guided to empty seats in the front row.

I met a Buddhist, Shifu Arakawa Tenshin. He was raised by the Dalai Lama's best friend from Tibet. Arakawa's a martial arts expert. He says that he'll see the Dalai Lama at his Wisconsin retreat. He says he's going to build a Buddhist center next to this Hindu center. We had several long and interesting conversations. Just meeting people of his caliber makes these gatherings worthwhile. I also briefly spoke with one of his students.

There was an energizing and uplifting evening Namasankeertan in the temple.

Tomorrow's concert is moved to the temple from the originally scheduled Buckmann Performing Arts Theater, because of storm damage.

Going back to Wayne's, I'm more centered and stronger. Negativity just slides off of me. I sent several e-mails, including my first to Luxmih, to be sure that I don't lose her e-mail address.

Saturday, August 2, 2003, I'm sitting in the temple with Bala, a nice, tall, young Indian from Memphis. This is his first time (these days) for Swamiji's Darshan. I tell him what I know of the schedule.

The evening's Namasankeertan session is one of the greatest experiences of my life. The sponsors are seated up front. I'm the closest one to Swamiji. Before the concert begins, Swamiji waves a huge crystal slowly from his right to left. I feel a wave of energy move with the crystal. The wave hits me with a powerful rush. Then with the first note of the synthesizer my third eye comes alive. I decide that I will use everything

I've learned over these many years. I use every mantra, pranayama or meditation that seems to fit. When Swamiji mentions the effect of each specific Raga, I concentrate on the body parts or consciousness that the Raga heals. My third eye remains alive. I am just energy and movement. Swamiji says that some of this music will be discordant ... I experience that part as a deeper healing into my spine. Once Swamiji looks at me and points upward ... I then take my consciousness to Sahasrar. Once I become too loud—Swamiji looks at me and gestures for me to quiet down. My back no longer hurts. I can twist and crack each vertebra at will. I'm stronger than I've been in twenty years. Swamiji says that it will take five to eight months for the back to heal—that we sit in chairs too much. Unfortunately, a month later, I briefly lost my discipline, and the back pain and limitation returned—if I had only known?

After the concert, one of the musicians comes up to me and shakes my hand.

Sunday, August 3, 2003, the last day's Yajna started a little early.

The Sri Chakra was performed and I was given my talisman, but it felt cold. Luxmih lost her card, so couldn't get her talisman. The thought came to me that my talisman might be meant for her, so I had her hold it. It felt hot to her, so it seemed to me that it was meant for her, so I gave it to her. She later bought me some items from the book-stall, saying that she felt drawn to do it. She also gave me a Japanese kimono she brought with her.

Swamiji performed the Maha Purnahuti of the Skanda Yajnam. Then the Abhishekam to Lord Muruga (another name for Skanda) took place. Swamiji said that he felt guided by Lord Muruga to come here. Swamiji said that he considered this as curious. Swamiji manifested Rudrakshas to Lord Muruga. There was a grand ceremonial procession of the deities around the temple. Local devotees have stated that this is the first time that there is so much jubilation in one of their Maha Yajnas.

The day's activities ended early and Swamiji left by car at 3:00 pm.

I had felt strongly, but illogically, to bring Band-Aids with me this time. Standing outside the kitchen, a woman hurriedly walked past me saying mainly one word, "Band-Aids." I said, "How many?" She told me and I handed them to her.

I got to spend several hours with my precious great-niece, Shanleigh. Shanleigh very fearlessly and gracefully rides horses. I gave her mother, Brittany, a large Rudraksha bead I was given at the closing ceremony. Brittany seems to want and expect something from me, and I feel honored to give her something.

Luxmih picked me up at Wayne's, and we ate at a Mexican restaurant. We spoke of Reiki, cranial therapy, Jann Thomas in Evansville (who she'd met), her going to China or Navaratri in India next, Kali Ray, martial arts, and my experiences at the Namasankeertan last night. I'm glad Wayne got to meet her, because it's much harder to call us a cult after meeting a stable lady like Luxmih.

Luxmih and I e-mailed each other after Memphis. In one e-mail, I mentioned a fascinating story in a recent newsletter about a miracle that happened later that month in New Jersey. Swamiji had manifested Vibhooti (holy ash) from a leaf garland. I had seen Swamiji do this several times before. But the really mind boggling miracle was that when giving the Vibhooti to the devotees, when the Vibhooti was running low, more would appear around the rim of the plate as if it was floating up to the surface from within the plate. Luxmih answered me by saying that she knew of this miracle, because she was the one carrying the plate!

Tuesday, April 13, 2004, at 5:20 pm, I left Evansville by bus for Baton Rouge. I had the names and birthdays of four people, to get Sri Chakra talismans for them: Lucille York, Maria Venturini, Thomas White, and the imprisoned Panchen Lama—Gedhun Choekyi Nyima. Swamiji had said to not underestimate the power of these talismans— that one was issued for Nelson Mandela before his release.

Three Amish people were on the bus. I read some in Swamiji's book, *Sri Chakram*. While others were sleeping, I did some of Swamiji's Kriyas and other mantras.

Although due in Baton Rouge at 3:00 pm on the 14th, we were forty-five minutes late. Jewell was waiting for me at the bus station. We then ate at Baton Rouge's only Indian restaurant.

We then went to Tunga's, where we would be staying. I met Tunga's daughters, teenager Holly, and five-year old Mahkayla. Tunga first met Swamiji in 1997, the year she first started doing yoga. She said that Swamiji probably saved her from a fire. Her dad worked for NASA in Italy and Turkey when she was small. Jewell has also lived in Europe.

Tunga and I had spoken at two other gatherings in years past, and participated in some of the same rituals. Later, looking through old notes, I ran across another time we had spoken.

I bathed late at night so I wouldn't interfere with the females using the bathroom in the morning.

Thursday, April 15, 2004, I was awakening to the soothing purring outside my door, by the beautiful cat, Shanti. They also have four kittens, three dogs, and a big white rabbit.

I got to speak, a little, with Mahkayla. We were talking about our favorite foods. I mentioned some fruits and vegetables, and then fish. She said, "You have to kill it."—she was sweet and pure, and tweaked my heart. Several years later I gave up fish.

At the Bhavan I spoke with some of the other devotees. Familiar and friendly faces, which I can't always attach a name. Including two American ladies that look so much alike, that I'm, kind of, developing a phobia about getting their names straight.

Dr. Rao spoke. Then Swamiji did Sri Chakra Puja.

Jewell and I went to a college hangout type place called the Coffee Call. Jewell went to college in Baton Rouge. The Coffee Call has this great tasting specialty called Beignet. It's a hot, puffed pastry, sprinkled with powdered sugar.

Back at Tunga's, I'm going to my room for the night. Little Mahkayla tells me, "Go to sleep when I do so you won't be all"—she then makes a gesture with her fingers cringed up like an attacker—"but"—she puts her hands in prayer pose—"calm for Swamiji." It was so sweet, and actually wise.

Friday, April 16, 2004, I had a nice breakfast, then off to the temple. More people now, as the weekend begins.

I spoke briefly with Luxmih. She's staying with Bhakti—I know who Bhakti is, but, as yet, haven't gotten to speak with her.

Dr. Rao says that Swamiji has a fever, sore throat, and twisted knee—that Swamiji probably will not be here today, but probably tomorrow. The children's program will be moved up to today.

I spoke to Laura, who I'd first met in 1997.

I bought a children's book for the kids in Evansville, a replacement tape for my damaged Celestial Message tape, and a meditation shawl.

I'm a sponsor for these events. I'm getting wonderful commemorative coins with engravings of the different deities. All, but one, still sit on my altar in Evansville.

I got to participate in the Sri Lalitha Sahasranama Puja. I recently (2008) decided to put the blessed rice from that Puja in the bush in my front yard, and also spend the three blessed pennies so that blessing would circulate.

The children's Bhajan competition begins. Swami Manasa is the judge.

Tunga's mother, Janet, stayed this night. She's an interesting woman with a strong, positive sense of family history. She's had Swamiji's Darshan.

Saturday, April 17, 2004, I woke to the first really full day—more people, more events.

Mahkayla gave me a hug. I juggled some rubber balls for her, and did my coin magic tricks. She started giving me points for my tricks, so I try and get better, each time. Sometimes, I jokingly argue, to try and get more points. Her mother says that she keeps saying, "Dyal did this, Dyal did that."

Tunga says that Mahkayla's name came to her as she was leaving the temple. That she had an earlier dream of a girl in pink with long black hair. She looked it up and found Maha Kala, but the priests told her that it's Maha Kali. When Mahkayla was little, Swamiji says to Tunga, "Where's Kali?" So, it's Mahkayla legally and Maha Kali spiritually.

Nothing officially scheduled in the temple now, but I go in to pay my respects. There's a private Puja going on in one corner. The participants graciously call me over. I fully participate—following the priests' instructions. I leave feeling elevated and strong.

During the Puja, I noticed a young woman in front of me that seemed to have similar back problems. I showed her a meditation that helps me. An older lady heard us, and asked me to show her. I showed her that one and some others, and then we spoke of many other things.

Laura's friend asks me if I have any news on Swamiji's schedule. I tell her what little I've heard.

I run into Narendra Dave and his family. Narendra and I shake hands.

The devotees from Newburgh are here.

Will says, "Hello, Dyal, how you doing?" I say, "I'm fine."

I'm in the food line. It's announced that Swamiji's coming at 4:30 pm. I eat, walk outside, and sit under a shade tree by the temple.

There I meet John Lentz. His name seems vaguely familiar. We begin talking. We ate at the same table when Swamiji was in Chicago in 2000. He was there from Maharishi's Maharishi University of Management in Fairfield, Iowa. Years later, I'm reading back issues of Bhakti Mala and find a fascinating article by John in the June 2000 issue.

It's announced that Swamiji will be here at 5:00 pm. It's getting very crowded.

I spoke more with John about TM, the Beatles, meditation, etc.

Jewell said that she wasn't being unkind by leaving for her errand for the temple without telling me. I told her that I never doubted her.

I talked to Ravi again. He's a student of Shifu Arakawa Tenshin, both, of whom, I first met last year in Memphis.

It's announced that today will be very different, but tomorrow will be as scheduled.

I got Tunga to write down Swamiji's car chant, and how to get a healing tea, she had mentioned.

Swami Manasa had a heart attack recently in Trinidad. Jewell had yet to hear of it. I was telling her how I found out about it, and I became so choked with emotion that I couldn't speak and my eyes watered some. I said, "Excuse me"—as I took my glasses off and wiped my eyes.

Waiting in the food line, there was a tiny girl hitting a boy twice her size. He did nothing. I patted him on the head, and told him that he did the right thing by not hitting someone back who was so much smaller.

We are all now waiting in the Bhavan for our turns to have Swamiji's Darshan. We are being called in by state.

I find a children's watch on the floor and discuss with others what to do with it. We decided to take it to the bookstall. Then later, I find out that I've missed the call for Indiana. I'm told to go in with the Dallas group.

Waiting with the Dallas devotees, there is a little boy out-of-control. I give him my notebook and pen to draw with. He calms down for awhile. Then I give him some of my blessed Himalayan water—with this he stays calm.

We're ushered in together, some fifty of us. A tall, athletic-looking, Indian man from our group speaks with Swamiji in an Indian dialect. Then the group leaves. A young couple and I are asked to stay. The couple has Swamiji's Darshan first. Then I walk up, in a state of deep surrender and humbleness. Swamiji looks at me and says, "It's OK." I get my blessed talisman and walk away. Then the clear thought comes from Swamiji to me, "Thank you."

Sunday, April 18, 2004, I'm sitting in the front row in the bhavan waiting for Sri Chakra. Mahkayla is sitting to my right, then Tunga. To my left is Julie/Jaya. Jaya took a picture of me with Tunga and Mahkayla, and said she'd send me a copy.

After Sri Chakra, Swamiji spoke. He says our heart should be in love with Krishna or Siva or Ganapati—it doesn't matter which one. He says that arguing is foolish—pick one path and take it all the way.

Swamiji manifested a necklace for a woman who had his Darshan from a video.

I received chakra talismans for all the people I had promised them to. The talismans came at once, but I clearly felt who each talisman was meant for.

Kaliji said to me, "Good to see you, as always." This was the first time I felt a strong, spiritual energy from her.

Swamiji released new T-shirts designed by Kaliji. Swamiji blessed the ones that people then bought, but I had already bought mine.

The Abhishekam of Datta and Anagha, Ganapati, and Siva was concluded.

Swamiji sat for a blissful, but short time, in silence with the devotees.

Swamiji blessed the bricks for the new Guru Nilayam. Daulet Sthanki and Harish Patel were entrusted with its construction.

Swamiji voiced appreciation for the Dallas devotees for donating the false ceiling in the Jayalaxmi Bhavan.

There was a rumor that Swamiji may come back tonight, even though all the scheduled events are over. I decided to stay, just in case.

I spoke some with Ean Lindsey from my 1988 Kriya Yoga Initiation Class. He works for the Attorney General's Office, was in Vietnam, and plans to retire on forty acres in Arkansas.

Dadaji was there again. I saw others approaching him respectfully, and bowing their heads. He would then place his hands on their heads. I did the same. There was warm healing energy in my head for several minutes.

I met an impressive young woman who is related to Swami Manasa. She confirmed that Swami Manasa did have a heart attack. She said that Swami Manasa is like a father to her.

One last meal is scheduled. An older, heavy woman does all the cooking, working long hours. She says she couldn't do it without Swamiji's blessing. A young man is her helper. Swamiji says that he is her son. He's lying on the floor, and looks to be asleep. The cook walks silently by him, to the kitchen. He immediately gets up and follows her.

Most of the devotees are gone. The priests lead an inspiring chanting session in the temple. Three chants that we do are: *Om Hreem Namah Shivaya, Om Dram Datta Yanamaha,* and *Om Sadgurave Namaha.* We also chant *Om Nama Shivaya* for Swamiji's health. They say that to give Swamiji rest is seva. Mahkayla was chanting. One of the priests says that the stars are Siva's mala, the ocean his shoulders, he talks through the Vedas, and the saints are within him.

At 7:56 pm, Dr. Rao says that Swamiji isn't feeling well and won't come.

I'm back at Tunga's. The smallest kitten is called Miracle. She was the last one of the litter. Jewell has gone. Tunga teaches her first massage class tomorrow.

Mahkayla asks me to tell her true stories. I told her of the rainbow cave in Spain, swallows in Capistrano, the little Hawaiian girl with Maharishi, and a little girl in Wisconsin who had a powerful mantra come to her. Then she asks me to tell her stories of Swamiji. I told her of seeing the Chakra with Swamiji in 1986, and several other stories.

Monday, April 19, 2004, Tunga goes to work, and the kids go to school. My bus leaves tonight. I do some housework, and collect and relay phone messages. Finally, I have a chance to do some necessary yoga. It makes me feel strong and clear. My back was very painful these days here—I need to do more physical yoga.

Tunga takes me to the bus station. I leave at 7:50 pm.

On my next bus connection, in New Orleans, there's a man sitting next to me that looks Mexican. We start to talk. He's Indian and from Swamiji's area. He knows of Swamiji, but has yet to have Swamiji's Darshan. He's blown-away to hear that I just left Swamiji. We talk through the night, from 10:20 pm until we catch separate buses at 5:45 am in Memphis. He taught me the Telugu alphabet. His name is Upendra Reddy. His mother and father were born in Nuzid, India. He's been to Swamiji's temple there. That temple was built by his grandfather's aunt. We e-mail often. He's moved twice, and I almost visited him once in Chicago.

Closer to Evansville, a young, under-educated girl leaving home for the first time, gets on the bus. She doesn't seem ready for the world. I give her one of the commemorative coins with an engraving of Datta and Anagha, telling her, "I have just left a high spiritual gathering, and you can have this. It has a protective element to it." She, very sweetly says, "Thank you."

Monday, June 13, 2005, at 6:45 pm, I left Evansville by bus to see Swamiji in Memphis. This is the Jeernoddharana Maha Pratistha, a grand reconsecration of all the temple idols. The Memphis temple idols are: Sri Venkateswara, Sri Devi, Bhu Devi, Sri Sita Rama, Sri Radha Krishna, Sri Ganesha, Sri Siva, Sri Durga, and Sri Subrahmanya (Muruga). This time I'm blessed to be a sponsor, so will have a car sticker to park close to the temple.

On the bus, I spoke some with a Buddhist from Cambodia. I read some of Swamiji and Swami Nityananda's writings, and meditated. Wayne will pick me up in Millington, Tennessee, just north of Memphis.

Tuesday, June 14, 2005, I have a free day with relatives and dogs before events start tomorrow at the Temple.

I spent a relaxing day with Wayne, speaking of many things, past and present; and had a heart-felt conversation with Wayne's boy Reid and Reid's girlfriend Chrissy. I threw a ball with Wayne's dog Marlene in the back yard, and slowly made friends with Reid's dog Dixie.

Wednesday, June 15, 2005, at the temple, Swamiji is received with Poornakumbha Swagatham by twenty-five temple priests from various parts of the United States.

Swamiji does Sri Chakra Puja, and the almost, continuous purification and consecration ceremonies begin.

As Swamiji's passing me, he says to me, "How are you?" I say, "Fine."—and then in a lower volume, "Nice to see you again."

After lunch, I had several nice conversations with devotees I'd seen at other gatherings.

I had a long conversation with Manu. He told me of when John Laird first invited Swamiji to the United States. He mentioned giving Swamiji two Tibetan prayer wheels, and the joy he felt when hearing that Swamiji kept one in the middle of his room.

I started having a headache near the end of the noon meal. It wasn't too bad, but lasted for several hours.

I met this very friendly, intelligent, American, devotee couple, Vandana and Ken Fries from Alabama. They were with a like-minded devotee from Georgia, Karen Goodrow. The ladies had been deeply into yoga for a long time—both had been to Kripalu.

My headache got frighteningly worse, worst when I was in the sun and heat. The head priest, Satyanarayana Charyulu, kindly took me into his apartment and gave me a head massage and a soft drink. There I met his sweet little granddaughter, Penate.

Karen told me about the lady saint, Karunamayi, who will be here Saturday. This will be the first time that I'll have the opportunity to have the Darshan of a lady saint. Karen has even seen her in India.

I had some free time that I could fit yoga into, so went into the Bhavan and did some of Swamiji's Kriyas, and several Sikh sequences.

I then sat down with my little notebook, to catch up with my notes. One of the ladies referred to me as "the writer".

I had a pleasant conversation with Kali Ray as we briefly held hands. Nice subtle spiritual energy.

Indian Classical Dance was the evening program. One woman and one man danced together combining Northern and Southern Indian styles—the fluid, precision movements are a joy to watch.

Swamiji spoke some but there was no Namasankeertan. Swami Manasa interpreted Swamiji's brief talk.

The dinner was Rajasthan cuisine.

Thursday, June 16, 2005, I'm back at the temple complex. The priests continue the ceremonies with the Agni Prajvalanam using the ancient method of "Churning and creating the fire in the wood." It seemed to take a long time.

I had a brief talk with a tall American devotee, Saraswati. I have seen her at several gatherings over the years.

I spoke some with Vishuda. He's an American devotee who I've seen at other gatherings. He's lived and gone to school in Indiana but now lives in Texas. Like most of the other devotees, he has led an interesting and insightful life.

I brought several copies of my "Epilepsy Cure"—spoke briefly with Swami Manasa about it.

My midday headache gets worse every day.

I got to spend more time with Vandana, Ken, and Karen. We have a lot in common. We still exchange e-mails.

There was a discourse and Namasankeertan this night. Many sang and danced in ecstasy. Each day there is a building in energy, yet each day is also full.

Friday, June 17, 2005, it's becoming crowded as the weekend people start arriving. I've already gotten more and deeper blessings than I expected, yet, in many ways, it is just beginning.

The homas continue with Adhivasas for the deities. The deities are spread out in front of the temple for devotees to have their Darshan. Abhishekam (ceremonial bathing) of all the deities takes place with milk, honey, curd, sugar, and ghee.

Swamiji says that Lord Venkateswara (the main temple deity)

removes sins and confusion. He says that thoughts, words and actions must be one. He says that we must return to our own Vaikunta some-day—that Atma, Shiva, and Vishnu are just a few of the many names of the Atman.

I ate lunch sitting with Vandana, Ken, and Karen. Karen has had the darshan of Swami Muktananda. This is the best meal, so far.

During the break, I manage to sleep for several hours on a couch outside the priest's quarters, but wake with the worst headache yet.

After something to drink, the sun going down, and sitting in the coolness of the temple, I'm better.

I met a very nice Indian man, Somya Gopalan. We relate as fellow devotees, with cultural differences between us as secondary—that's the way it should be.

Earlier, in the temple, I noticed this stunningly beautiful woman sitting some ten yards from me. I just turned and focused on the events, wanting to keep my spiritual perspective. Not likely that I'd see her again, as it's getting increasingly more crowded. The next temple event, she's sitting just five yards from me, and again I just turn my attention to the program.

Then today, I sit in the back on one of the few chairs, trying to save my back and knees. Next to me is this friendly, perceptive, Indian devotee. We talk for a few minutes, then she leans back to introduce me to her daughter, who's sitting next to her. Her daughter is the beautiful Indian. They are such wonderful people, and the daughter is as gracious and perceptive as she is beautiful. I know that these exceptional women are a great blessing when I am clear and only an obstacle when there is something wrong with me.

I sit on the floor, so someone else can have my seat. Vandana has a book of the chants—which makes it much easier. The Namasankeertan is great, but the pain in my back takes some away from it.

The dinner is under a huge tent. I sit with three Indians. We talk of Tai Chi, hatha, Guru Purnima, and many other subjects. The food is great, but I have to hurry so I'll be waiting when Wayne comes to pick me up.

Saturday, June 18, 2005, I'm back at the temple, and drink the herbs from the morning Sri Chakra Puja.

The idols are brought within the temple for reconsecration. There is great jubilation and ecstasy among the thousands now present.

Swami Manasa spoke, then Dr. Rao.

The lady saint, Karunamayi, arrives. She is accompanied by a drummer. She sits on the dais next to Swamiji. There is obviously deep respect between them. They speak together for a short time, and then Swamiji yields the stage for her to address us.

She mixes chanting and speaking. She has an angelic voice that deeply penetrates. She says there is one God and the saints are his rays. She says that she is coming to us as our own mother … this brings me to tears. Others around me are also crying. She speaks highly of Swamiji's music. She says the Dharma is absence of hate—is love … Swamiji nodes in agreement. She also says: Giving is living. ♦ Ganesh is Sachchidananda. ♦ When selfless we are immortal. ♦ The self is Omkara. She performed several chants—one to Ganesh.

Swamiji spoke briefly—addressing Karunamayi as Sri Mata.

Karunamayi left the stage, moving slowly through the adoring crowd. Prasad kept asking people to move back and give her room. Karen told me later that Karunamayi said to her, "See you in India."—and Karen replied, "Yes."

I spoke again with Swami Manasa and gave him a copy of my "Epilepsy Cure".

I sat on a bench outside the temple, and did a lot of yoga, including chanting the Hari Krishna Chant sixteen times. Swamiji had said earlier that if we do this chant sixteen times, twice a day, for seven days, the Sadguru will answer our question—or if we are in silence for two days.

I met a nice young man with a Southern accent. Krunal's his name. It took me awhile to realize that he's Indian. The world sure is getting smaller. Krunal is from Bombay, but went to high school near Memphis, and is studying business in Mississippi.

I got to spend a few minutes with the head priest's granddaughter. She's a bright and sweet little girl—she seems (and rightfully so) more comfortable here than anyone.

There's a inspiring and uplifting evening Namasankeertan.

I saw Dinesh Sthanki from Baton Rouge. He gave me his e-mail addresses.

As I was out of money, I left a copy of my "Epilepsy Cure" as an offering for Swamiji.

Sunday, June 19, 2005, I woke at 3:30 am on very little sleep— fresh and ready to go. Once at the temple, at 5:15 am, I bowed respectfully to each of the idols.

Today, Swamiji will perform the Maha Samprokshana to Venkateswara. The remaining Kumbhabhishekams will be completed by the other priests. There will be grand processions with trumpets and jubilation. Swamiji will be hoisted to the roof of the temple on an electric lift.

I spoke more with Kaliji. She says when receiving Swamiji's thoughts, a feeling of peace comes with it—that doing alternate breathing before can help. We touched hands again and she leaned her left shoulder towards me. I put my right arm around her shoulder and massage it gently—it all felt very pure and natural, but we were both surprised I did it.

Vandana says that Ramakrishna told his disciples that it takes twelve years of celibacy to achieve the Siddhis (the ability to perform miracles). This came out of our discussion on transmuting our life force for spiritual purposes.

My headache came back, but this time I was dizzy and felt I might pass out. I went into the kitchen and talked the cooks into giving me some Chai tea and a banana. Logically eliminating causes for my sickness, I came to the conclusion that it was because I had recently allowed a doctor to talk me into taking niacin. I stopped taking the niacin, and the headaches stopped.

Swami Manasa leads the chanting, and then the Baton Rouge priests lead.

Penate gently tapped me on the shoulder, and then waved to me when I looked at her. I said, "Hi, sweetie." She sat beside me for a while and then left saying, "Bye, bye."

Swamiji speaks, and Swami Manasa interprets. Swamiji tells a man to meditate at Lord Venkateswara's feet and his dead son will appear.

I spoke again with Mohan and Purnima, the Indian couple I sat with at Saturday's dinner. I gave them my e-mail.

I'm walking by the bhavan, and hear my name called. Turning around, I see the beautiful Indian lady and her mother waving me to them. I go inside and sit. We speak of many things, spiritual and mundane. We talk of string theory—the beautiful Indian is as smart as she is beautiful. I mention the Himalayan water I have from Swamiji. They say that the United States puts too much extra into our water.

At one point, I catch myself saying something really goofy. I'm obviously thrown off balance by the stunning beauty. No one speaks, and then we go on as if it didn't happen.

Then I sat in the temple for a long time, talking with Karen. We told each other our guru stories. She told me of studying under Swami Muktananda and Brahmananda Saraswati.

Then at 4:30 pm there's devotional music by Mrs. Shobha Raju from Hyderbad. She sings bhajans by Annamacharya. She turned down offers to sing commercially. Her strong, yet sensitive and penetrating voice brings joy to the hearts of the audience.

Swamiji comes. Shobha Raju still sings awhile longer. I'm sitting on a chair in one corner of the temple. Karen is to my right. Swamiji is sitting against a wall, directly in front of me. I try and connect to Swamiji every way that seems to fit. I do the first four of Swamiji's Kriyas. I dig deeper, do the direct kundalini technique, mantras and meditations—all the while being as silent and unobtrusive as I can, so as not to disturb others.

Awards are given to the priests. Different people make speeches. I have to leave before it's over, because Wayne will be here soon to pick me up.

Monday, June 20, 2005, I woke at Wayne's and got ready to go to the bus station.

I spoke briefly with Wayne's wife, Dean. I gave her my condolence on the passing of her son, Mark, who passed last year of MS. Dean and I hugged.

Wayne told me that when Mark's daughter, Shanleigh, heard of her dad's passing, she went in the back yard to be alone. She heard someone calling her name. She then went back into the house, and complained about someone calling her name, as she had told them that she wanted to be alone. Then she was told that no one called her. Some of us believe it was Mark calling his daughter.

When I first heard of Mark's passing (we were very close), I thought to him that I was sorry that I didn't do something he wanted me to do when we were last together. Then I heard a voice say, "It's all right."

On the bus ride home, I gave out several copies of my "Epilepsy Cure", one to a guy from England.

Friday, July 15, 2005, 2:58 pm, I left Evansville by bus to attend Swamiji's "Music for Healing and Meditation Concert" in Youngstown, Ohio. I felt powerfully drawn to attend this concert—that Memphis had been a blessing and Youngstown will be the seal that makes the blessing permanent.

I barely had enough money to go—purchasing the most expensive concert ticket.

A young guy gets on the bus and sits next to me, against the window. His face looks like he's recently been beaten up. I decide not to talk to him. Necessary small talk happens, and he seems mannerly and intelligent, so I change my mind. He says his name is William F. Cody III and he's the great-nephew of Buffalo Bill Cody. He says this is the cause of his recent fight, and many others—that when men in a bar find out who he is, they often want to fight him. This seems realistic, particularly since he can real off all of Buffalo Bill Cody's ancestry.

I change buses in St. Louis. I do the first four of Swamiji's Kriyas, and easily feel more subtleties from the Kriyas than I have previously. I feel how they fit with Sri Chakra … my awareness is lifted and strong, and I am incredibly high. Just this experience makes the trip worthwhile.

July 16, 2005, at 10:15 am, I arrive at the Youngstown, Ohio, bus station. The ride was long, and I feel very grubby.

I found Kilkawley Center, where the concert will be, on the campus of Youngstown State University. Then I went back to a Taco Bell to eat, relax, and decide what to do next.

The restaurant manager tells me that most of the university is closed. This makes me feel really bad, because I really need to clean up before the concert. Then he says that he thinks there's something going on in Beeghly Center on the campus.

I walk through the deserted campus and find Beeghly Center. There's an unlocked door—I walk in. At the end of a long hall, I hear faint voices and see a few people. Looking for a place to clean up, I walk past a sign that says "Family Rest Room". Not sure what this means, I open the door and walk in. There's a small room with lockers, and another room with a shower, sink, hooks to hand clothes, a mirror, and a toilet. You can even lock this room from the inside. What a blessing—I clean up and leave, even shave. Describing this to someone later, she says that Swamiji's looking after me.

I walk around the campus—finding places to read, meditate, and do the Sikh Spinal Sequence.

Inside Kilkawley Center the concert is to be in the Chestnut Room. I arrive early, so I can get a good seat and socialize.

Outside the concert room, I'm happy to see Luxmih from Memphis of 2003. Swami Manasa embraces me on the shoulder as he walks by.

Inside, I get a great seat, about six rows back, next to the center aisle. Luxmih is in front of me. Behind me is this fascinating old yogi from New York, Pitambar. He's an encyclopedia of American yoga history. I'm very pleased to see Karen, from Memphis, come and sit next to him. Vandana and Ken are also here.

During a percussion solo, Swamiji walks among the audience. When coming to me, he touches me on the shoulder saying, "You're doing fine." His healing energy is warm and subtly strong. His words feel more like a statement than a question. Then he walks back to Luxmih and gently taps his knuckles on her head. Then he turns to me again, touching my shoulder, with even more and deeper healing warmth. I could feel this energy for several hours.

During part of the concert, the mantra *Aham Brahmasmi* was floating effortlessly through my mind.

My bus doesn't leave until tomorrow. Vandana and Ken graciously allow me to stay with them at Motel 6 for the night. They played Swamiji's CDs as we engaged in fascinating discussions, both spiritual and mundane. Vandana says that my psychic abilities are evolved.

They drop me off early at the bus station. I have four hours to wait.

The bus station has a full time security guard. Her name's Mary—we have long and interesting conversations.

Finally on the bus, I meditated when I could and gave a *Dattamala* to an Ethiopian woman.

I missed my connection in St. Louis and was stuck there all night. The girl working the counter said it wasn't safe to go outside. I spent my last dollar buying corn chips.

This kindly Vietnam vet bought me some food, saying, "Us old guys have to stick together." I gave him a *Bhakti Mala* as I left him in Evansville.

Chapter Fifteen: Karunamayi, the Compassionate Mother

Sunday, May 7, 2006, I'm on my way to the Sri Ganesha Temple in Nashville, Tennessee. Karunamayi will be there for three days. It doesn't look like I'll get to have Swamiji's Darshan this year. It's much easier to get to Nashville, and Swamiji clearly gave his approval of Karunamayi last year in Memphis.

Karen has told me a lot about Karunamayi since Memphis, and I've looked into Karunamayi's Web site.

Before Karunamayi's birth in 1958, the revered saint Ramana Maharshi broke his usual silence to tell Karunamayi's mother, a humble devotee of his, that she would give birth to the Divine Mother. Thus was born, Bhagavati Sri Sri Sri Vijayeswari Devi, also known as Karunamayi, the compassionate Mother, or simply Amma (Mother).

Though never having studied Sanskrit, when Amma was very young she amazed Sanskrit scholars, who were visiting her home, with her deep metaphysical insights.

She once cared for a maid who was desperately ill with cholera, disregarding her own safety. To the delight and amazement of her family, the servant recovered quickly, despite the doctor's dire prognosis.

As a young woman, she spent a decade in the remote and sacred Penusila Forest meditating and performing spiritual practices on behalf of humanity. "When I was in the forest," she explains, "meditating in silence, the vibrations of the mantra I was inwardly chanting affected the wild animals. Cheetahs use to come, and sometimes one would put his head on my lap and sleep. Small deer would come and pull my sari. In meditation, when we become one with nature, the animals, plants, and trees, become one with us and cease to behave in the normal way. In this wild forest where I did penance, there was not a single day when even an ant bit me."

Parrots and other talking birds picked up the words of her chanting; she speaks of walking through the jungle hearing them singing "Om shanti" and other mantras. Since that time, at the ashrams she founded in Penusila and Bangalore, as well as in her travels to the West, she has devoted herself to bringing peace and God consciousness to the world.

I stayed at a Howard Johnson, just two highway exits from the temple's exit. The clerks were Husein and Harry. Harry was an Indian from Bombay. Harry said the Sri Ganesha Temple was not his main temple, but he still graciously gave me a discount as I was leaving.

It is 2:42 pm; I'm at the temple early. The only thing scheduled today is an Evening Program at 7:00 pm. At the bookstall, I met two devotees from California, Brett and Ram Das, who are traveling with Amma. Brett is the percussionist during the chanting. Ram Das has been following Amma for six years. Several priceless books and CDs— books of metaphysical knowledge that I could spend a lifetime studying, and CDs of Amma chanting holy mantras and even explaining the correct pronunciation. I have yet to have Amma's Darshan, but the trip has already exceeded my expectations.

I met several other devotees, including an Indian lady who is married to an American. She's studying medicine at Vanderbilt. She spoke of meeting Satya Sai Baba in India around 1980. I gave her some information on the Memphis Temple.

I talked to a calm and informative devotee named Surya. He says that Amma has been considered, for a long time, as an incarnation of goddess Saraswati.

Amma arrives. To her right is a large poster of goddess Saraswati, the source of language, and the arts. Saraswati sits on a swan and plays the vina. To Amma's left is a large poster of Lord Siva—the source of all potential and destroyer of all unneeded weeds.

There's a projection screen with wonderful sayings. Amma speaks on topics of great substance and depth. With my maximum attention, I can still only absorb a small portion. Amma teaches the Saraswati Mantra: *Om Aim Srim Hrim Saraswati Devai Namaha.* The good works she is doing in India, for the poorest of the poor, melts everyone's heart.

We stand in line for a brief Darshan, after the discourse. When it's my turn, I walk up, feeling incapable of speech. Amma says, "You like fruit?" I say, "Yes"—and receive my piece of fruit. Amma says, "See you tomorrow"—not as a question, but telling me the future. As I'm walking away, I say, "Thank you, Mother."

Monday, May 8, 2006, 8:42 am, I'm sitting in the same room in the temple as last night. Today's schedule is Individual Blessings, 9:00 am–12:00 noon. Karen said that this and tomorrow's homa are the strongest events for her.

We're sitting in chairs and given instructions for the Darshan. We're told that Amma only sees good things—that she knows our needs, so we don't have to be overly detailed—that the only problem she sees is our lack of God realization or Moksha. We write down our questions, because it feels good to express them.

We're given a numbered card to write our questions on—told we can mention the reason we came, blessings needed, problems we need help with, and any goals and desires. I write my name on the top of my card and: problems with back pain, problems with knee pain, and blessings for my meditations.

We are to approach, and bow with our hands in prayer pose. We'll be given Vibuti (holy ash). We handle the Vibuti with the thumb and ring finger of the right hand. The Vibuti is put on the third eye in the morning after bath and before the meal, also in the evening. We are not to share it. The altar is a good place to keep it, not on the floor or in the bathroom. It was said we'd also get kumkum powder to put on the third eye—that it gives power and protection, and the ability to see future karma coming. It should be kept with us. I didn't get some this time but have at other times.

We'll also be given a card with Amma's photo on one side and three mantras on the other side. One of the mantras, Mrutyunjaya, was once a secret. We can share it, but it is a healing mantra for outer use only—we cannot listen to it when not in activity. It's good to listen to or chant this mantra when cooking. Another mantra is the Saraswati Mantra from last night. The third mantra is Gayatri. I have heard of it for years, but didn't want to get the pronunciation wrong, or have it without the blessings of a saint. I had heard that without these two prerequisites the mantra wouldn't work, and may even be a handicap when the conditions are met later. Amma has books and CDs on Gayatri and may even be chanting it tomorrow in one of the homas. It was said that we should chant the mantras, at least, twenty-seven times a day—that once a mantra is memorized it is constantly vibrating inside us.

Photos and sayings are on a large screen. They come and go faster than I can write them all down. Some are repeated. Two I catch are: "If you come one foot towards me children, I will come thousand feet towards you."; "Your Faith is your greatest protection. If you have Faith, you have everything."

Amma arrives at 10:12 am. She chants part of Sri Suktam while offering milk over a large Sri Chakra. She says that doing Gayatri in the sun is healing.

We do several chants that are on the screen. In one we lift our hands up to feel the energy.

We all wait quietly and patiently, as we're brought up by rows for our Darshan. There are mostly Indians here.

My turn comes. I place my card on a tray, walk up to Amma, kneel, bend forward, and close my eyes. There is a lot of pain in my body, at this time. Amma gently strokes my forehead ... waves of bliss roll through me. I clearly feel where the waves hit tension, I relax the tension, and it leaves. As the last knot of tension dissolved, Amma stops the massage at that exact moment.

Amma gives me a Durga talisman that she says I am to keep in my wallet. Durga rides a lion and manifests to destroy evil. There is nothing stronger than Durga.

Amma hands me back my request card, with a vibhuti packet, the card with her photo and the mantras, and three small Hershey Chocolate Hug candies. I leave, sit down, and wait.

I had noticed on Amma's Web site that she comes back, shortly after leaving, to talk with the few who stay. So, I sit, and wait.

Amma leaves after the structured Darshan, and then returns in a few minutes. There are some fifty of us sitting at her feet. She speaks to the group and a few individuals. Devotees get close to her and bow as the opportunity presents itself—yet still trying not to be too pushy. My chance comes. I get close, and Amma says to me, "You are my son." I bow to her. She touches the top of my head. The healing warmth is even stronger than at the structured blessing. I am in ecstasy ... there are no problems.

I got the directions to tomorrow's homas.

Tuesday, May 9, 2006, today's homas are in the backyard of a private residence on Polo Club Road. Not as many people as in the other events. We're sitting in chairs facing the homa pit that sits under a tall tent.

There are seven successive homas. The first is Sri Ganesha Homa, which removes obstacles and brings success. The mantra is one I've been familiar with for years, and chant often. Amma says that doing this mantra at night removes the day's karmas.

The second is the Sri Saraswati Homa, which bestows knowledge, creativity, and memory. This mantra is the one I just learned two days ago. Amma says doing these holy mantras once in this environment is equal to doing them a thousand times elsewhere. I have attended homas in other traditions, but here there is much more explanation.

Next is the Sri Gayatri Homa. The first vibration is Om, the second is Gayatri. All things come from Gayatri. Gayatri explains everything. It increases spiritual energy. The best time to do it is 3:30 am–4:30 am.

The fourth is Samputita Sri Suktam Homa. It is Goddess Laxshmi, honorable wealth on all levels. She is the consort of Vishnu. It's good to do this worship in front of Sri Chakra. It's also good to do it with the sunrise.

We are given some Mudras and visualizations—are told to say the names of people that we want to receive blessings from the homas, except relatives, who automatically get the blessing. Wonderful clarity and elevation is happening—I see where this is one of Karen's favorites.

Fifth is Sri Guru Graha Shanthi Homa, which rectifies imminent and adverse astrological transits.

Sixth is Mrutyunjaya Homa, which gives physical, mental, emotional, and spiritual healing. This is the one that Amma says was once a secret.

Last is Sri Devi Homa, which bestows divine grace, protection, and spiritual upliftment. This is done the last three days of Navarati.

Amma says that the Poornahuti, at the end, is as good as all the other rituals combined.

We all wait in line for a short Darshan from Amma. When my

turn comes, I come forward with my hands in prayer pose, and bow respectfully. Amma puts holy ash on my third eye and says, "I love you very much." I leave with warm energy at my third eye that I relax and surrender to, so that it will stay longer.

Then there is a delicious outdoor Indian meal.

I met three other American devotees who have also been doing yoga for many years. Fred Statile has been doing yoga for thirty-one years. He was living in Hawaii but is now in New York. He's been following Amma for six years, or so.

Robin Fuller very kindly took pictures and said she'd send me copies. She said that she thought I'd like that. She did send me copies, and they are very good ... helps me take my consciousness back to a better time.

The other devotee is Brenda. Brenda and Fred have been TM initiators for twenty years.

Sometimes we got a little confused when talking about Amma and another lady saint, Ammachi.

I decided to stay another night and get a fresh start in the morning.

Back at the hotel, I couldn't get to sleep. I was even getting a horrible headache—with one of the new mantra CDs playing, this seemed irrational. I left my room with an apple, water, some of the new books, and my notebook. The lobby was closed, and it was too cold outside. I found a warm and well lit stairway.

Being too tired to read, I close my eyes to relax, and maybe meditate. After several minutes, I'm alert. Looking inside, I clearly see a triangle of light at the base of my spine. I relax more, surrendering deeper, hoping this will make the vision stay longer. Usually my visions are very short, a second or two. This one stays for ten or fifteen minutes. The triangle has colors, but when I write the vision down later, I can't remember what colors.

The vision fades and I go back to my room. The CD has ended, the room is normal, and my headache is gone.

Wednesday, May 10, 2006, I woke to a fresh clear morning, bathe, and do some physical yoga and meditate. Then I go to the hotel lobby for a breakfast of coffee, orange juice, and a bagel with cream cheese.

Looking through my notes, I realize that I couldn't sleep last night because the Mrutyunjaya Mantra was playing. That's the healing mantra that can only be played during activity.

Saturday, June 16, 2006, I left for St. Louis to see Amma. My traveling companions are Carey Smith and Julie Little. They both went with me in 2003 to see the Dalai Lama in Bloomington. Carey also went with me in 1998 to see Swamiji in St. Louis at this same temple.

We stopped about half way there and ate at Applebee's in Mt. Vernon, Illinois.

Once there, I took Julie inside the temple. Dr. Naidu was beginning to give a Westerner a tour of the temple. I asked if we could join in. Dr. Naidu accepted. Great timing, as Dr. Naidu briefly explained each of the idols. Then Dr. Naidu and I spoke of when we were both here for the Foundation Stone Laying Ceremony in 1990. I mentioned to him the story I'd heard, that when Swamiji first came in 1990, others voiced concern about the excessive rain ruining the Foundation Stone Laying Ceremony. That Swamiji then waved his hand across the sky, and it didn't rain till after the ceremony. Dr. Naidu then told me that he was there, and witnessed Swamiji wave his hand. Dr. Naidu said he would send me photos of Sai Baba of Shirdi (which he did). I was thinking that a vision I once had was of Sai Baba of Shirdi, but when the photos arrived, I realized that it wasn't him.

Outside, we met a few people, including a Christian monk from Washington, D.C.

Amma's Evening Program was upstairs in the Mahatma Gandhi Center, which is in front of the temple. She showed these wonderful detailed slides of the chakras, while verbally giving even more details— fascinating information which I couldn't completely follow, much less write down. We chanted the Saraswati Mantra, then "*Om*" nine times, then a silent meditation. The silent meditation in Amma's presence is often more powerful than chanting aloud. She stressed the importance of being without thoughts, for spiritual growth.

One of her devotees said that these screens had never been shown before.

There's a brief Darshan after the Evening Program. When my turn comes, I walk forward and bow. Amma says, "God bless you, my son."

I'm handed a banana. When I walk off my banana catches Mother's sari. I say, "I'm sorry." Mother and her devotee helper giggle in unison—it's a sweet moment.

That night Carey, Julie, and I eat at a nearby Waffle House. Nothing unusual happens, but my senses are heightened, and my mind is calm and clear, without the usual intruding and useless thoughts.

Saturday, June 17, 2006, Carey and I are at the homa. We're sitting in the front row of chairs, and saving a seat for Julie—she left to get something to eat. Julie comes back.

The homa begins—same as in Nashville but with some differences in explanation. When speaking of Ganesh, Amma says that he is the kundalini. She says that "*Gam*" is his seed mantra, and we should meditate some on this mantra. When she says this, "*Gam*" feels much stronger and clearer than any other of her words. Amma says that Sri Chakra can accept any puja. She says that one spoonful of Ghee (purified butter) a day can destroy any poison.

This time I understand a little more, and have some clues about what else I must learn.

There are some fifty people sitting on the ground between Amma and us.

When we're not following some instructions or chanting a mantra that I can follow, I'm focusing on the spine and thinking "*Gam*". Then for a few blissful seconds, I clearly fell/see mantras coming off of my spine.

After the homas, there's a meal and free time to socialize and buy more at the bookstall.

Later, Julie told me that Amma said to her, "Beautiful, beautiful, beautiful."

Monday, April 30, 2007, at 6:06 pm, I left Evansville by bus to see Amma in Memphis. The last couple of years I have been slowly sinking—health problems, willpower, energy, and joy of life declining, though interspersed with short periods of happiness. Amma's presence and teachings have lifted me back up. I now have memorized some of her shorter mantras—which I chant often. Some of the longer chants, I'll chant along with Amma on the CDs. Her books enrich me, almost daily.

In Memphis, the priests will be performing Ashtottara Satakundatmaka Ashtamukha Gandabherunda Narasimha Mahayagnam to prevent natural calamities, restore balance in nature, promote understanding and tolerance among the nations and various faiths of the world, and for universal peace. This yagna will be conducted by 108 Agama Pundits in 108 homakundas.

It's a pleasant bus ride. I met Jack Hunt, a sort-of latter day hippie. Another guy, a long-haired professional drummer who has some interesting stories, and I can't forget the carefree man who misses his gun and his horse.

Tuesday, May 1, 2007, at 1:30 am, I arrive at the bus station in Memphis. My brother Wayne's there to pick me up. Wayne's a retired Naval Intelligence Officer. After some needed sleep, I'll have a full day with relatives before the temple events start tomorrow.

I wake leisurely, eat breakfast, and talk with Wayne. I get some computer time, send a lot of e-mails, and make some chess moves on my Internet matches.

Wayne's wife Dean gets home from work. Wayne's boy Reid and Reid's new wife Chrissy come over. We have a nice meal.

Reid has a new dog, Jack. Jack sort-of adopted Reid. It's fun to watch the three big dogs chase each other in the hilly back yard.

Wednesday, May 2, 2007, I'm at the temple at 7:30 am for the start of the first day's events.

By the priest's quarters, I met a friendly priest called Ananda. He's from Livermore (San Francisco). He said, "The body is God's."

In the temple, there's an early morning ritual in front of Lord Venkateshwara. I get in line with everyone else. The temple's head priest sprinkles holy water on me as he says to me, "How are you?" I say, "Fine."—it's nice to be recognized.

I follow the others. A metal helmet is placed on everyone's head. Small prasad, blessed food, is given to each of us as we put out our right hands and bow slightly. Later, I hear that this was for the priests only.

Amma leaves Lord Venkateshwara's inner sanctum and walks slowly between two lines of devotees. As she gets to me, she smiles, nods, and gently touches me on the head as I bow.

I met Irmhild Bettenworth. She's German, but is now living in North Dakota.

I was delighted to see Somya from 2005. He now wants to be called "Sam"—I guess that's easier, but I was getting to like saying "Somya". This time, his family from India is here. His wife is Sreedevi, son is Krish, and daughter is Tejazvi. They are a very delightful family.

Sam and I were both initiated into the Babaji lineage. Sam has a Ramakrishna photo he may show me. Sam is a speech therapist and speaks Tamil, as does his wife. They seemed to like my yoga stories, and I certainly appreciate their spiritual companionship.

At the bookstall, I spoke to Brett and bought a Sri Chakra and a meditation shawl.

Back at the temple, the priests are doing wonderful Sanskrit rituals. My left foot is swollen some, and pain is increasing. I go in the back and sit in a chair and stretch—this makes it some better. Several months ago, I had to be hospitalized for this, but I thought it was completely healed.

The priests are presented with robes.

I go off by myself so I can do healing meditations. They help some.

I come back and sit as close to Amma as I can. The pain has spread to both legs and my back—I'm getting frightened.

There's a small line of people seeking Amma's Darshan. I get in the back of the line. One of her helpers tells me that this line is for the priests only, so I sit down out of the way, but as close as possible. The pain is increasing—I'm almost in tears.

I notice some non-priests in the line. Amma nodes to me, indicating I can come forward.

I approach and kneel. Amma says, "Love you so much"—as she touches my head.

I say, "Mother, I am having trouble with my legs—it's hard to be here."

Amma touches my head again as she says, "Don't worry, I will help you. Love you so much."

As I rose to leave, I noticed that I had been resting in Mother's lap.

I now know that I'll be alright.

We chant "*Govinda*" … it is blissful.

The evening meal is Rajasthani. I spoke some with a man I believe is the father of the beautiful Indian girl from 2005. We had spoken some years ago. When I told him my name he did a double take.

Thursday, May 3, 2007, 8:21 am, I'm back in the temple complex. I meditated some in the Homa Shala. Only a few priests are here, preparing for the homas that will start soon. Large, inspiring paintings of Gods and saints line the inside of the Yaga Shala, also beside the road coming up to the temple. I took a few photos of them.

I met Steve Thomas from San Diego, California. He's been following Amma since 1998. We sit together most of the time. I pick up a lot of valuable, or at least interesting, information from him.

I met several other people who I had pleasant conversations with but can't remember their names.

Steve and I found good seats close to where Amma would be sitting. When Amma arrived, I bowed to her, and she smiled and nodded to me.

Sam and Sreedevi approach Amma for Darshan. Sam doesn't get close enough. When Amma reaches to bless him, he's too far away.

When Sam and Sreedevi leave, I rush up to them and tell them what just happened.

I met an American devotee from California, Peter, and his small son.

The 108 Homa Kundas are starting—Sanskrit mantras, fire and offerings. I'm sitting with Steve and a few other American devotees—surrendering, just thankful to be in this holy environment.

During the break, I went with Sam and Sreedevi to their apartment. They were very gracious. We had Chai, sweets, and nuts. Sreedevi gave me a Venkateshwara Murti and a Sri Rudram CD that she got in India. The Venkateshwara Murti still sits on my altar, and is one of my most prized possessions.

Sam showed me his altar and spoke of his spiritual linage. He also showed me this great Web site connected to his lineage.

Back at the temple complex, I'm sitting in the meal tent so I can prop my feet up. Most people are in the nearby Yaga Shala.

There are storm clouds overhead, so I decide to go early to the bhavan where Amma is scheduled to speak in half an hour. Once there, I'm the only one in the bhavan. I get a good seat, stretch some, and relax. Then a thunderstorm erupts. Slowly people come in. I'm the only one who didn't have to deal with the rain. This impeccable timing lasted the rest of my days here. When I had something I wanted to do, when Amma was scheduled to speak, I would do what I felt to do, get to the event late, and shortly Amma would arrive. I didn't have to strain—I would always be on time, even when late.

Amma arrives. She says that Sanatana was the name of God before the Vedas. Gayatri is the main life nerve for the heart.

Amma touched my third eye and the top of my head.

I met a woman named Jean. We talked of our respective pain pills. She offered to give me one of her extras. I thought about it for a long time, and then decided not to take hers.

The evening meal was Tamil Cuisine.

Friday, May 4, 2007, 8:16 am, I'm back at the temple, then to the Homa Shala for the morning homas.

I'm not a sponsor this time, so am not allowed to sit next to the homa fire and toss the offerings in while chanting the mantras. Though, sometimes, when one of the homa fires doesn't have a sponsor sitting at it, non-sponsors will be asked to fill in.

Although I'm still in some pain, I know from past experiences, that when being closer to the healing fires, the pain can lessen or even leave completely. So, when I get the chance, I do sit in.

This time, I do get to sit in. At first my pain is decreasing, and then it slowly returns, and even gets worse. Now I am in obvious distress, shifting continuously to try and find a position I can bear. During a break, some of the priests come up to me and ask what's wrong. My legs are now visually swollen. One of the priests, Ananda from Toledo and West India, gives me concrete suggestions, so I zero in on him. I do the exercises he shows me. He says he'll show me more on the next break. I find him on the next break and get more exercises, asking him to repeat details as I write everything down. I have done these exercises every day since, and even passed them on to others—the swelling has not returned.

Amma comes. She touches me on the left side of my head as I bow.

There's now turmeric water by the Yaga Shala that we put our fingers in, and then sprinkle the water on our heads before entering the Yaga Shala.

I now spend more time off by myself, so I can stretch and meditate.

I did my coin magic for some of the little kids. One of them called me "Uncleji" and another called me "Magic Uncle."

I heard that a lady here had a vision of Lord Narayana during this retreat; Narayana is the focus of this yagnam. Years ago, I woke up one morning alert, but with my eyes closed. Inside me, for a few seconds, I am Lord Narayana, lying flat, in perfect peace, in an ocean of bliss. While here in Memphis, I sometimes remember this vision while looking at the posters of Lord Narayana. Once the vision returns, though even shorter, and this time there is also some movement ... very subtle ... yet, very real.

Amma says that Lord Narayana was called here by our hearts.

I have been e-mailing friends while I'm here. It feels like I can somehow communicate the inexpressible when I'm actually in this holy environment.

Now, I'm just standing outside the bhavan between events. It's getting crowded as the weekend people begin to arrive. The weather is perfect. To my far right, someone is walking quickly towards me. The person walks in front of me, and turns facing me—it's Karen! I said, "Give me a hug" and we hug. I catch her up on what's happening here, and we are together during much of Amma's remaining time in Memphis. Karen's very knowledgeable about what's happening among current American yoga devotees, and has even been with Amma in India.

Saturday, May 5, 2007, I arrive at the temple from a different direction, as we had to first drop the dog off at the dog grooming shop.

There are wonderful homas, more people, and a more festive atmosphere. I'm usually sitting close to Amma, with Karen and Steve.

I walked up to a group photo that was being taken of the priests, and was motioned, as were others nearby, to stand in, in one of the photos. Amma smiled at me, and I could clearly feel an uplifting effect for some fifteen minutes.

An older Indian devotee came up to me and said that I should help these two Americans that had just come, and seemed unsure of what to do. I walked up to the two American women, introduced myself, and told them what was happening, some of the inner significance, and what the protocol is. Their names are Rhonda and Monica. They're friendly, open, intelligent, and seem to be on a mission. I tell them that to touch Amma's feet, gives you the Shakti (spiritual juice), and is a great blessing.

As Amma walks by us, the women hurry to get in front of her. As Amma stops, the women prostrate, and touch Amma's feet. It is a pure and holy moment.

While standing with Rhonda in the Homa Shala and explaining who Amma is, I had to stop in midsentence and turn away or I would cry. Amma is a Goddess among us, no words can describe her greatness.

Later, Amma is sitting on her throne and giving Saraswati Mantra initiation to children and students. Among many other things, Saraswati gives memory, so this is excellent for students. The children/students stick out their tongues, and Amma writes the mantra on their tongues with a small stick.

I quickly look for Sam, Sreedevi, and Peter, so that they can get this great blessing for their children. I finally find them, all together, a few yards from the Homa Shala. The children have already gotten their initiation. The children, in turn, stick their tongues out to show me. It's very precious, makes me smile, particularly when little Tejazvi does it.

Karen said that a few years earlier she also got this initiation. She just got in line with the others, and when it was her turn Amma went ahead and gave her the initiation. Only later did she find out it was only for children and students.

In the evening, Dr. Shobharaju, a spiritually elevating vocalist, performed. She said that Amma manifested a Krishna Murti for her.

I ate the day's meals with Karen, Steve, and Peter.

Sunday, May 6, 2007, I'm riding with Wayne to the temple. He says his granddaughter, Shanleigh, says, "Hi." I say, "That's not fair", for now, I have to stay over an extra day to see her.

I take my newly purchased Sri Chakra and the Venkateshwara Murti that Sreedevi gave me, with me to the temple, so that they'll be more energized when I put them on my altar at home.

Although I can't now sit at the homa fires, I am close enough to participate in some of the ending rituals. A gracious, older, Indian lady makes sure that I'm included. I do small offerings, some chanting, fit in when I can, and move when I'm in the way, as do many others. Sometimes, I'm even helping direct others, as processions move around.

Amma says that the merit from this yagnam will last for seven generations … that this particular yagnam has not been done for many centuries. The priests here are like walking Saraswatis. To namaskar (place hands in prayer pose) to Amma makes energy move from Amma's feet to our hands. Truth and humbleness are necessary to reach Saraswati.

We all, very powerfully, blissfully chant the mantra "Gobinda." Amma says it means ananda or bliss.

I get to speak some with Peter's wife Madurai. She's like a flower unfolding. Their son's name is Josh.

The top of my Sri Chakra is chipped. Madhuri thinks that I should exchange it. I'm not sure when it happened. I take it back to exchange it, but they wouldn't even consider it.

Sam says that the water brought over in the ceremony has Narayana in it. Sam has seen Lord Narayana manifest, twice.

Monday, May 7, 2007, I'm staying over an extra day, so I can see Shanleigh and her mother, Brittany.

I get to see Shanleigh ride a horse over an obstacle course. She is impressively graceful, and from a distance looks like a miniature adult.

I feel out, if they are open and ready for a Sri Chakra. Although since it is chipped, I can rightly call it just a pretty crystal. Shanleigh seems open and ready, so I give her the crystal. I also give some holy ash from the yagnam to Brittany.

May 2, 2008, I'm going with Manna Wightman to Nashville, Tennessee, for Karunamayi's Darshan. Manna and I went to Bloomington in 2007 to see the Dalai Lama. Manna called the night before to confirm that it's not a dream, and that I will have enough money, and that I'll have hot Chai tea, and a Basmati rice dish waiting for her in the morning.

We left very early. Pickles, Manna's car, drove well and fast, although he looks like he's on his last legs/wheels.

Time passed smoothly as we were usually chanting in the car. I was astutely aware of my brain. I could easily relax any tense part, and would then feel increased energy flow both inside and outside of the brain.

As we got close, pleasant memories of my other time at this temple came rushing in. We pulled into the Sri Ganesha Temple, then directly to the Darshan room. Just a few minutes late, we sat in the first empty seats behind the others, about three hundred people. We were given cards on which to write our questions to Amma.

The people in the first row stood in the aisle, waiting for their turn for Darshan. I told Manna the procedure and how the requests were to be put on the cards. On my card I wrote: Dyal Roberts; help with will power; help with meditation; help with back, knees, and skin; anything else Amma sees I need; I feel blessed just to be here.

The line was moving very slowly, so I went to the bathroom and back. The line still hadn't moved much. I noticed that people were putting items on a tray, and when their time came, the tray was brought to Amma to bless. I went to the bookstall and bought a crystal Sri Chakra and a jade Siva Linga to be blessed. Then I gave Manna money so she could buy her own Sri Chakra. Such an incredible opportunity, for when these holy murthis are placed on one's own altar, they are a continual blessing.

I had to bring a cane this trip as my knee and back were worse. Standing for a long time could greatly increase the pain. I mentioned this to the lady who was in charge of the waiting lines. She said she would help me. When it came my row's turn, she moved me up to the front so I wouldn't have to stand as long, but it still was long enough to greatly increase my pain.

The tray with my Sri Chakra and Siva Linga is brought to Amma … she blesses them.

I walk up to Amma and bow. She says, "Is your health bad?" I say, "It comes and goes, but would be good if I was with Amma all the time." Amma says, "You are my son … grandson." Amma strokes my head, and healing waves flow through my head, through my arms, chest, and stomach, into my legs, then it stops.

Amma hands me a new card with Amma's photo on one side, the

same three mantras on the back, two or three Chocolate Candy Hugs, and a packet of holy ash. I walk away pain free.

After me there is a break. Manna's turn will be soon, when we start again.

I take Manna upstairs to the actual temple. She is impressed.

Standing by the bookstall, I see two little kids outside, through the glass wall. The boy hits the girl. I tap on the glass to get his attention, and then wag my finger at him. The little girl gives me a smile that melts my heart.

Back in the Darshan room, Manna has her turn. The Darshans are finished, Amma leaves, and I go up to the large Sri Chakra that Amma was using for worship. With my hands held above the Sri Chakra, I feel strong soothing energy.

When Amma returns, a small group of us go to sit at her feet. I'm having some difficulty sitting on the floor. Amma motions to me and says, "Sit in chair." I move a few feet back and sit comfortably in a chair.

Amma speaks to the group as a whole, and sometimes to individuals. She tells Manna to make everything like a puja (a holy ritual), like when cooking. She says that to teach people to connect to God, will stop suicides, but we must keep it simple. Discipline comes from God. Food is energy. The Sri Suktam of Goddess Laxshmi creates a golden radiance that protects from the negative effects of Saturn. Spiritual people have a responsibility to guide the world because politicians know less.

Later, outside, we were there when Amma and her entourage packed the van and left. We were in the group photo. Amma looked at me when saying that we should come to the healing session to be held soon in Memphis. One of Amma's entourage said that the healing they'll do in Memphis is very powerful … with him saying this, I felt a strong, clear, energy, telling me to go to Memphis.

Tuesday, May 6, 2008, 6:05 pm, I left by bus for Memphis. I will again stay with my brother. There will be a Sri Panchakshari Sahita Mrityunjaya Yagnam. This Yagnam is to promote world peace, prevent natural calamities, and decrease epidemics and accidental or untimely deaths. Being for Lord Siva, this yagnam excites me very much, because

I know both of the mantras they'll be emphasizing, Mrutyanjaya and Siva Panchakshari, and had a vision of Siva when with Swamiji in Baton Rouge in 1995. Rituals start on the seventh although Amma isn't scheduled to be in Memphis until the ninth. Because of Amma's previous schedule ending midday on the seventh, I'm hoping that she'll be early to Memphis.

This time I keep my cane with me, because my left knee is swollen and tender. I have difficulty standing for long periods, although I can usually walk without the cane. Two nice women see my difficulty and save me a good seat on the bus.

I gave one of Amma's brochures from Nashville to a nice lady named Ann Arnold. It seemed meant for her, as I didn't need it for this trip and didn't know I had it.

I also met a young woman from Memphis who is related to Elvis—she even looks like him. She told interesting stories, and wasn't afraid of leaving the bus station in Memphis late at night.

Wednesday, May 7, 2008, the first day at the temple starts at 5:00 pm. Wayne and I ate at a Mexican Restaurant. Wayne was surprised when I decided to pay. I save all year for these holy events.

When I'm finally at the temple, the feeling is "I'm home." The head priest and Dr. Duggirala speak kindly to me. The head priest tells me that Amma will be here tomorrow night, although it's not on the schedule. I notice that Dr. Duggirala is now simply called "Dr. Prasad." That's fine with me, as I never got the correct pronunciation of Duggirala. The head priest addressed me as Mr. Roberts.

An older Indian lady that I've seen many times greeted me warmly as we held hands. Then she was a little confused as to who I am. I smiled and was friendly, as I've been in her shoes several times.

I took the yagnam vows and had the yellow string tied to my right wrist. I vowed to: be here all five days, be celibate, sleep on a hard surface, and have no meat or alcohol.

I managed to sit on the hard marble floor in the temple and felt strong energy running through my hands.

I got to drink some of the holy water from one of the rituals.

This is the highest I've ever felt at a gathering before the saint even arrives.

Amma is Brahma for this yagnam. She's in charge, sees that it's done right.

Thursday, May 8, 2008, is the first full day at the temple. Wayne and his wife thought it was goofy of me to sleep on the hard floor last night, instead of their new bed. Besides a few priests, I'm usually the first person at the temple. I can meditate in the cool morning air, and spend blessed quiet time worshiping the idols.

I walked into an early morning ritual at the Venkateshwara idol. Only one priest, a couple, an older devotee, and I were there. I got to touch a tray of flowers and say my name. The priest then repeated my name with some mantras. At the end of the ritual, a metal hat was put on everyone's head. Then I was given a ripe banana, which I really needed.

Sreedevi is here. She introduces me to her friend Tai. They do the seva of making the Homa Kundas. They also make Siva Lingas that line the walk to the Yaga Shala. A few days later I actually feel energy from their Siva Lingas. I once joke with them and another devotee that it's like the Siva Lingas that just appear in mountain streams in the Himalayas, although, once said, it didn't feel like a joke.

Anil Kumar came up to me. He remembered me from Baton Rouge when Swamiji was there. Anil's from Memphis.

Sam introduced me to his friend Balaji. Balaji is one of Lord Vishnu's names.

I'm in the Homa Shala looking for a place to sit. There's a wood crate next to me. Dr. Prasad says, "You can sit. It'll take the weight."

I stretched when I could, and tried to stay out of the rain and mud. Once, I was blessed to get holy ash for my third eye.

An Indian lady, who just arrived, asked me the schedule and where each activity would be held.

I met Satya from Arkansas. She remembered me from last year. I mentioned to her that since her name means truth and mine means compassion, together, we would be an unbeatable combination. She was with Irmhild Bettenworth, from North Dakota, who I had spoken to last year. I later took a photo of them in the Yaga Shala and sent them copies, as well as some other photos I'd taken here.

Steve, from last year, is also here. He said he saw Karen in Atlanta and she mentioned that I might be here. I reminded him of Karen's name. Nice friendships developing in this small but universal fellowship. I tell Steve that because of my bad knee I won't try and sit at a homa pit this time.

I went to the building where the food is prepared, to use the restroom. A bashful little girl looks at me and says to her mother, "Magic Uncle is coming."

Just after leaving the building, I pass Dr. Prasad. He says, "Dyalji, Mataji is coming. Go stand by number six." I reply, "Thank you. Thank you, very much." Realizing how much this means to me, Dr. Prasad says, "You're welcome."

I walk up to priest quarter number six, place my cane around the corner, and wait by the door. Some thirty devotees form two separated lines for Amma to walk between to get to her quarters.

Amma gets out of the car and slowly greets and blesses each devotee. When almost to me, she turns facing the other line. I clumsily try to bend and touch her feet. No one is looking at me. I catch my fall with my left hand, and place my right hand lightly on Amma's left foot. I'll never forget that touch.

Amma is in her quarters. Someone comes to her door and says that Amma would like us all to come in. We crowd into the small doorway. Sreedevi is trying to get between the bushes and the crowd—I reach out my arm to help her.

Once I'm inside, Amma motions for me to sit in a chair opposite her. Others are sitting knee-to-knee on the floor. I'm so happy. Tears of joy are welling up inside me … as they are even now, just remembering this holy moment.

Amma passes out fruit. I receive an apple with my right hand. A crate of mangoes is brought to Amma. I'm not sure if it's proper for me to get a mangoe also. As I'm thinking this, Amma says to me, "You can have a mangoe too." I walk up to her and receive a mangoe.

Devotees are bringing luggage. I'm sitting on the floor. I'm thinking I may be in the way. A devotee tells me he can walk behind me. Sam and Sreedevi come in, as does Peter from last year. Many have short conversations with Amma … being respectful. A few leave, so I leave also.

I feel highly blessed, yet Amma isn't even scheduled to arrive until tomorrow.

I connected Satya to an Indian lady, through Sam, who will help her get some Indian clothing.

In the evening there was a Bharatanatyam performance (Indian dance).

The meal line was longer than I first thought—it twisted again once you got close. My knees were hurting too much—I had to sit down. Sreedevi came up to me, as did Ganesh Ramachandra. Ganesh got some food for me.

Awkward, but now I feel safe. Then Sreedevi tells me that one of the dishes I've eaten a little of has eggplant, my allergy. I mention this to Dr. Prasad. He sends another man to get me some medicine. I take the medicine and don't get sick.

Friday, May 9, 2008, I'm at the temple a little early, because Wayne has a dentist appointment. I use this opportunity to take some photos of the mesmerizing large posters of the deities and saints that are inside the Yaga Shala and on the roadway up to the temple.

I chance upon Amma's official photographers taking a group photo of the priests. I walk between the photographers to a perfectly centered open spot. The photographers finish, and the priests stay a few seconds while I get my shot.

I spoke with several devotees, and then went to Amma's discourse in the bhavan.

Amma led transcending chants, including Mrutyunjaya, Ganapati, and Aham Brahmasmi. She says that anyone helping us is God. It ended with everyone lining up for Amma to put an orange paste on their third eyes. When my turn came, Amma says to me, "Thank you for coming, my baby, thank you."

I got to spend the afternoon break with Sam and Sreedevi at their apartment. I needed to call my doctor, but couldn't reach him—which was good, because I would have just found out that I have skin cancer that has to be removed. The worry cold have hurt my attitude here, when it wound up that just a simple procedure removed it all.

Their altar and their stories of the deities and saints were uplifting.

Sreedevi fixed us some Chai tea. Sreedevi was surprised to hear that Amma's incarnation was predicted by Ramana Maharshi.

Sreedevi and I had a pleasing conversation on the long ride back to the temple.

Peter's wife, Maduri, is here now. I spoke more with Steve. He said that googling Khadgamala gets good results. I tried it later, and he was right.

I'm with Amma in the bhavan. She motions to me to sit. She leads us in chanting: *Om Namah Shivaya*. I've discovered that sitting on the floor when chanting is physically healing for me. Dr. Prasad says Amma's Ashram is the kundalini of the world and the source of life. Amma leads us in chanting *Om* and the *Ganapati Mantra*. She says that playing *Lalita Sahasranama* when going to sleep gives peace.

At the end, Amma tells a story of a couple that argues often. She gives them activities, and the arguing stops. As Amma's leaving, she turns to me and says, "You have time to quarrel?" I comically reply, "No, no time," Shortly, I realize that this is something I need to use in my life, now.

Saturday, May 10, 2008, I'm at the temple even earlier today. Sam, Sreedevi, and Satya are here.

Amma starts speaking in the temple around 8:00 am. She's walking around some, and everyone's standing. Very little English is spoken. It's extremely difficult for me. I'm learning how to tighten my body to lessen pain. When she says a mantra, I start thinking that mantra. Sometimes, I'm the closest to her. Several times she glances at me.

Now, back in the Yaga Shala, I have pleasant conversations with Steve and Madhuri. I'm too close to a speaker and the hot sun is now on me, so I move to the back to sit on a chair in the shade.

The lunch break is starting. I hurry to the path leaving the Yaga Shala, so that I have a chance of having Amma's Darshan. As she gets to me, she says, "After meal, go sit in the Yaga Shala to do meditations." What a blessing, to have direct instructions from a saint, so naturally, I obey. She said the same to Steve, who was just in front of me.

I'm back in the Yaga Shala after lunch. I meditated, as Amma ordered, and I clearly needed it. This time in the Yaga Shala there are very bright lights which attract bugs, so, I have another reason to sit on one of the chairs in the back.

There's a very cute, little girl charming everyone in the back, as she pretends to knock bugs off of people. For a while, she's by this young Indian woman, who has the most hypnotic smile I've ever seen.

I notice an American woman standing at the Yaga Shala entrance. She seems confused. I walk up to her, and ask if I can help. Her name's Susan Warmack Fondren.

This is her first time, but she is open and sincerely searching. We go to the bookstall where she buys a few items, and then to her car to snack. I tell her the schedule and how to maximize the benefits of being here.

There's a very interesting and powerful, psychic dynamic between us … shifting quickly and unexpectedly between old friends, fellow seekers, teacher-student, and strangers passing with no contact. Quite a challenge to adjust, let go, and then come back together.

Susan and I made it to Amma's Darshan. I introduced her to a few people. Amma speaks. She says that we should chant the Saraswati Mantra five times, and then sit in silence, focusing at the third eye—that we should increase the time in silence. Amma leads us in the Ganapati Mantra. She says "Sri" is divine light, conscious light, supreme truth, Laxshmi. Ghee controls pollution. Amma feels the effulgence of Lord Venkateshwara, here, especially here, though God is everywhere.

There was a short Darshan at the end. I waited for Susan. She came to me beaming, saying Amma told her she loved her. Susan and I hugged.

The Indian woman with the hypnotic smile sat close to me. I could only recognize her when she smiles.

Wayne met Steve, Sam and Sreedevi. The more contact he has with these normal and even exceptional people, the harder it is to call us a cult.

I did get to see my great-niece, Shanleigh, and her mother, Brittany. I gave Shanleigh an un-broken Sri Chakra. After I explained it briefly to Shanleigh, she told her mother, "It has energy." I also gave them pieces of a blessed apple.

Shanleigh is an accomplished equestrian and wants to ride in the Olympics. She's ten now, but has been riding since five.

Sunday, May 11, 2008, I'm back at the temple for the last day's events. Today will end several hours earlier than the other days. There's an early Parvati Puja for Amma, because she's sick.

The temple's Siva Linga came out of the crate with a natural crack that looks like the moon.

Arathi is the most important—without it, the ritual has no effect.

Steve missed last night's Darshan, so I got his e-mail to tell him what he missed.

I was outside the Yaga Shala as Amma got there this morning. She said, "The wind is blowing your hair"—as she moved the hair from my forehead.

Once, inside the temple, the lines leading up to an idol were imbalanced, with only the priests on one side. I got on the side with the priests, and then others followed suit.

I finally got two of the mantras correct. Steve said the same happened to him.

I met one of Amma's traveling entourage, Shawn Frances Patrick O'Brian. He had studied directly with Swami Rama. I told him of my vision of Swami Rama, as told in chapter eleven, and later, of my friend from Ireland who could see the Little People when she was young.

I did my coin magic for some of the children.

I met a very nice American devotee, Smriti Dudley. I helped her take some photos by steadying the posters while she shot them.

Another American devotee, named Jan, kindly asked me how my knee was doing. Jan's very dedicated in doing her silent mantra repetitions.

The temple is very crowded today. I strained some trying to sit.

Back in the bhavan, Mother gives her last discourse. The wonderful priests are felicitated. Amma says that deities with many heads, means that they help in many ways. She says that only courageous people speak the truth. That the Goddess takes different forms to fulfill our different needs, but she is the same omnipotent Mother.

Speaking to the congregation as a whole, Mother says, "Write this in your book: *Laziness is the Enemy.*"

Resources:

Karunamayi:
   http://www.karunamayi.org

Ganapati Sachchidananda Swamiji:
   http://www.dattapeetham.com
   http://www.dycusa.org

Yogi Ramaiah:
   http://kriyayoga.org

Dalai Lama:
   http://www.tibetancc.com
   http://www.dalailama.com

Baba Ram Dass:
   http://www.ramdass.org

Bhante Gunaratana:
   http://www.bhavanasociety.org

This autobiography tells of the unique journeys (outward and inward) and the otherworldly visions of a '60s hippie, growing from the carefree communes and rock festivals into the timeless wisdom of the great mystics of our age.

Dyal takes us through his experiences with the gentle Buddhist Monk, Bhante Gunaratana.

Then we meet Baba Ram Dass, the American Yogi, previously known as Richard Alpert, who was fired from his teaching position at Harvard for working too closely with Timothy Leary on his LSD experiments.

Next we travel through California and Europe with Maharishi Mahesh Yogi, the early guru of the Beatles.

Then we're introduced to the American Yogi, Swami Rudrananda.

Pir Vilayat Khan, the Sufi (mysticism that includes all religions), takes us to a depth of reality few Americans even know exists.

We then travel to the Colorado mountain retreat of Swami Amar Jyoti.

Next we experience the power and incredible depth of insight of the Sikh master, Yogi Bhajan.

Chapter eleven is the Dalai Lama, Ocean of Wisdom, whose presence and techniques help us overcome our real enemies … our inner afflictions.

In *Stray Visions and Insights* are experiences that don't fit into the other chapters, but are worth mentioning.

Then, we are enriched by a vision of the mythical Himalayan master, Babaji.

In the next chapter we learn of Sri Ganapati Sachchidananda Swamiji, the Great Master.

In the last chapter we hear of Karunamayi, the lady saint whose incarnation was foretold by the revered Ramana Maharshi.